Fourth Edition

Arrshath Mohaideen.
Level 4.

weekendLearning
Series

Islamic Studies

Level 4

Mansur Ahmad and Husain A. Nuri

Weekend
Learning

Copyright © Weekend Learning Publishers

ISBN: 978-1-936569-15-1

First Edition: 2008
Second Edition: 2009
Third Edition: 2010
Fourth Edition: 2012
Reprint: 2014
Reprint: 2016, 2017

Cover Design and Photography: Mansur Ahmad

Illustrations: Mansur Ahmad, Husain A. Nuri and Reza Al-Amin

Weekend Learning Publishers
5584 Boulder Crest St.
Columbus, OH 43235
www.weekendlearning.com

Printed in China

Preface

The concept of a series of Islamic Studies books was conceived in 2002 when both of us were teachers or principals of two weekend schools in two different states. We used several excellent textbooks and reference books in these schools. However, we soon realized there was no single textbook available that could meet our classroom needs. Some of the available books had too many or too few lessons for an academic year. Some lessons were too long for a class hour, and some were too short. Some lessons were too difficult for the ages involved or too basic for higher-level classes. Some books were not written with a 12 year curriculum in mind. The lessons in higher grades, therefore, did not develop from the knowledge base of prior years. Sometimes, extra emphasis was placed on one topic at the cost of other important topics. Thus, we thought a balanced knowledge base was lost.

We always felt there was a better way. We began writing the lessons ourselves to meet the needs of our schools. We involved other teachers in this process. For the next two years, we conducted classes based on the lessons we had prepared. In the meantime, both of us met with other principals and teachers across the country. We wanted to find out how they taught Islamic Studies and what their major concerns were. Most of the principals and teachers we talked to expressed their inability to find or develop a good curriculum. If they had a curriculum, they could not find lessons to complement the curriculum.

This survey prompted us to develop a functional, comprehensive curriculum for weekend schools in the West. We wanted to create a curriculum that would include everything that Muslim students growing up in the West would ideally need to know. We wanted to include topics based on the life experiences of students growing up in the West. Muslim children growing up in the U.S., Europe, and Australia are facing diverse challenges and conflicting pressures at schools and in social circles. They are constantly influenced by the mainstream youth culture. We wanted lessons to address their issues from their perspectives.

The curriculum alone would not be of any use unless there were lessons based on the curriculum. The lessons had to be age-appropriate and suitable for the typical class duration of most schools. As we continued to write and edit lessons over the next two years, we discovered ways to make the curriculum increasingly meaningful.

In 2007, we published coil-bound versions of these books. More than 30 schools in the U.S. and UK used the books. We also received a large number of inquiries from many other schools. Based on the suggestions, comments, and reviews received from many of these schools, we have edited the series of books and made other changes as appropriate.

We are thankful to Allāh for giving us the ability to write these books. We pray to Allāh to accept our labor and make us successful in communicating the message of Islam. We hope Islamic schools and home schools in the U.S. and other countries will find these books useful. Any errors in the books are our responsibility. We appreciate receiving meaningful comments and suggestions to improve the series.

"Our Rabb! Accept from us, you indeed are the all-Hearing, all-Knowing." (2:127)

January 15, 2008

Mansur Ahmad
Husain A. Nuri

Preface to the Second Edition

Alhamdulillah, the second edition of the book is now ready. Second edition gives us the scope to improve the text, presentation and format without sacrificing the overall ease of use and appeal of the lessons. We have reformatted the homework section to make it user friendly.

We thank all the teachers and home-schooling parents for adopting this and other books in the series. We are especially grateful to Oure Marvel for reading the text and suggesting various changes. Her acute attention to the details was helpful in preparing the second edition. We are thankful to Zafar Azam of Khatoons, Inc., for his valued advice and guidance to print the book in color. We are thankful to students, teachers and parents for their continued support. We hope this edition, too, will receive similar recognition from weekend schools, teachers, students and parents. May Allāh accept our small effort.

July 15, 2009

Mansur Ahmad
Husain A. Nuri

Preface to the Third Edition

In the third edition of the book, we made small changes and improvements in the book. Several lessons now have a Points to Ponder section to encourage critical thinking.

We express our thanks to Allāh for giving us time, resources and ability to continue working on this and other books in the series. We are thankful to students, teachers and parents for their continued support. We hope this edition, too, will receive similar recognition from weekend schools, teachers, students and parents. May Allāh accept our small effort.

October 15, 2010

Mansur Ahmad
Husain A. Nuri

Preface to the Fourth Edition

All praise is due to Allāh alone. We are indebted to Him for this book and other books in this series. It is because of His grace that in a relatively short period of time, the fourth edition of the book became due. In this edition, we have made a few changes in the text, illustrations, presentations, and layout without sacrificing the overall ease of use and appeal of the lessons.

We are grateful to Brenda Rusch for editing and proofreading the book. She has not only eliminated a few grammatical, punctuation, and spelling errors, but also improved content flow, transitions and overall organization. We thank Shamim Nuri for her assistance during the production of this edition. We also thank all the teachers and home-schooling parents for adopting this book and other books in the series. May Allāh accept our small effort.

August 15, 2012

Husain A. Nuri
Mansur Ahmad

Table of Contents

How to use this book effectively
Instructions for teachers and parents

The lessons for fourth grade Islamic Studies are designed to provide basic information on Islam. Like the other books in the series, this book also begins with a few topics on Allāh (swt). The key events of Rasūlullāh's life (S) are spread out over eight lessons. These are followed by short histories of the Four Rightly Guided Khalīfahs. Prophets Hūd and Sālih (A) are introduced this year. Interesting Facts are included in some of the lessons to impart knowledge about the creations of Allāh, and to also make a connection between the *deen* and the *dunya*.

For maximum benefit, each lesson should be completed within one class hour. We recommend that a test be conducted after every fifth or sixth lesson. Weekend Learning has designed an Excel-based user-friendly program to record homework assignments and exam scores. It will be very useful when report cards are prepared. To obtain this program, as well as question banks, ready-to-print exams, and homework questions, please order a CD from the publisher.

Homework:

Teachers are requested to regularly assign and grade homework. The time commitment for homework is about 10–15 minutes per lesson. The homework is designed to reinforce the material learned in class and to develop a regular study habit. Frequent supervision of homework by a parent will indicate that education is valued.

Regular Interaction with the Qur'ān:

Every Muslim student should develop the habit of interacting with the Qur'ān. To complete certain homework assignments, an English translation of the Qur'ān is strongly recommended. The purpose of such homework is to build a strong connection between the student and the Qur'ān. Insha-Allāh, such homework will plant a seed in the minds of children to continue a life-long interaction with the Qur'ān.

Teaching Respect:

From an early age, students should be taught to show respect to Allāh, His angels, and prophets. In order to encourage respect teachers and parents are requested to mention the following:

Whenever the word Allāh appears in the book, please add the glorification "*Subhāna-hu wa-Ta'ālā.*" Whenever the word Muhammad, or other words indicating Muhammad, (for example Rasulullah, the Prophet, or Nabi) appear, please add the prayer "*Salla-llāhu 'alaihi wa Sallam.*" We have used (S) throughout the book as a reminder of the prayer. Whenever the student reads the name of a prophet or an angel, please add the prayer "*Alai-hi-s Salām.*" This is noted by (A). Students should be taught to add the prayer "*Radi-allāhu 'an-hu*" for a khalifa or a male companion of Rasūlullāh (S). For a female companion, the prayer "*Radi-allāhu 'an-hā*" should be used. These are noted by (R) or (ra).

Suggestions:

Please provide any suggestions, corrections, ideas, and so forth, to improve this book by sending an e-mail to the publisher at weekendLearning@gmail.com. It is a combined effort of the publisher, authors, teachers, and parents to prepare our future ummah. May Allāh guide us all! Amin.

Rewards of Allāh: *Everybody Receives Them*

Objective of the Lesson:

As Muslims we must try to receive rewards from Allāh. His rewards are given in this life and in the Hereafter. This lesson discusses what the rewards are, who can receive them, and what we can do to receive them.

When we do a good job, we expect a reward. Teachers reward us when we do well on an exam. Parents reward us when we do something great. Sometimes the rewards are simple words of encouragement or sometimes a gift. When we do something that pleases Allāh, He rewards us, too. His rewards are not words of admiration. He rewards us with something that benefits us. His rewards are the Best Rewards.

Rewards are for everyone: Allāh rewards everyone. Rewards are not limited to only a few people or to human beings alone. Allāh rewards animals and plants, too.

Rewards in many forms: Sometimes we receive gifts for no particular work. The water we drink and the air we breathe are such gifts from Allāh.

We receive some rewards for working hard. For a farmer, the reward for taking care of the crops and the garden is a good harvest. When we study, we receive rewards in the form of good grades in school. After finishing college we will get a good job. With the money we earn, we can buy a house, food, and clothes. All these things are rewards for working hard.

All these rewards exist only because Allāh gives them to us. He is the Best giver. Sometimes He gives rewards in the form of happiness or joy. Sometimes He gives rewards in the form of health and peace of mind. When we spend money in Allāh's way, He multiplies our wealth.[2:261]

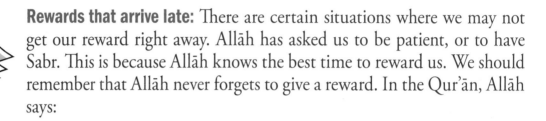

Rewards that arrive late: There are certain situations where we may not get our reward right away. Allāh has asked us to be patient, or to have Sabr. This is because Allāh knows the best time to reward us. We should remember that Allāh never forgets to give a reward. In the Qur'ān, Allāh says:

Certainly those who recite the Book of Allāh, and establish the Salāt, and spend out of what We have provided them with—secretly and openly, they can hope for a deal that will never run out. (35:29).

When prophet Ibrāhīm (A) and his son, Ismā'īl (A), built the Ka'bah, they prayed to Allāh to accept their effort. Thousands of years later, Allāh rewarded this prayer by making the Ka'bah our Qiblah (the direction in which we pray). This reward is so great that over the centuries, billions of Muslims have made their salāt facing the Ka'bah. Prophet Ibrāhīm (A) and Ismā'īl (A) made this du'ā:

$$رَبَّنَا تَقَبَّلْ مِنَّا ۖ إِنَّكَ أَنتَ ٱلسَّمِيعُ ٱلْعَلِيمُ ﴿١٢٧﴾$$

Rabbanā taqabbal minnā. Innaka anta-s samī'u-l 'alim.

Our Rabb! accept from us. You indeed, You are the all-Hearing, the all-Knowing. (Al Baqarah 2:127)

Some rewards are in the Hereafter: When our lives in this world are over, the good people will go to Jannat, or Heaven. This is the ultimate reward. We all must work hard to get this reward. This reward will not be given unless we qualify. We cannot even imagine how grand Jannat will be. Our reward in Jannat will be more than what we want.[50:35] Once we are in Jannat, we will stay there forever.[98:8]

And as to those who believe and do good, We shall let them enter Gardens under which flow the rivers, living in it forever. For them there will be in it pure companions, and We shall admit them to a dense shade. (4:57)

...dy can take away your reward: In school or while doing chores we do a lot of good work. ...we do not always get recognized for our work. With Allāh, our good is work always ...ed. Our good deeds are always carefully recorded. There is no chance that our reward may ...o someone else by mistake. It is also not possible that someone can take away our rewards.

...āh (swt) will not run out of rewards: If everyone at school receives a reward or a medal for ...me kind of good work, there may not be enough medals for everybody. However, Allāh's ...wards never run out. His reward is not like a medal in a game that only one person receives. ...llāh can reward as many people as He wants.[3:27]

You do not have to ask for rewards: Allāh is watchful over everything. Even if we do not ask Him, He rewards us for every good deed. The reward is always better than the good deed.[27:89] If we ask Him, by making a duʿā, He may give us much more than we ask for. Allāh teaches us many duʿā in the Qurʾān, and many are listed in the books of Hadīth.

How to get Allāh's rewards: We all want to get rewards from Allāh. Some of Allāh's gifts are free—such as air, water, and the environment. The best rewards are not free. We must earn them. We can earn these rewards by obeying Allāh, obeying our Messenger (S) and following the guidelines given in the Qurʾān and the Sunnah of the Messenger (S). Sunnah means the examples of the Messenger (S).

1. Name four gifts that Allāh gives us even if we do not ask for them.

    1) _____

    2) _____

    3) _____

    4) _____

2. Name four rewards that Allāh gives us when we work for them or pray for them.

    1) _____

    2) _____

    3) _____

    4) _____

3. What is the best reward that will be given in the Hereafter?

_____

4. Circle T if the sentence is true Circle F if the sentence is false.

Allāh gives rewards only to human beings, not to animals.   T   F

The rewards of Allāh are always in the form of money.   T   F

Nobody can take away our rewards from Allāh.   T   F

Allāh can give big rewards to anybody He wants.   T   F

5. Using an English translation of the Qur'an, read verse 4:79. What is the source of any good thing that we may have?

_____

6. Memorize the duʿā of Prophet Ibrāhīm (A) and Ismāʿīl (A) as given in this lesson. Be prepared to recite the duʿā in front of your teacher in the next class.

Discipline of Allāh: *Because He Loves Us*

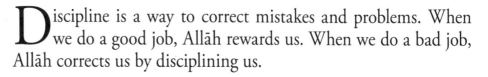

Objective of the Lesson:

Allāh often disciplines us to make us better in our efforts. The purpose of discipline is to make us realize our mistakes, overcome them, and work to improve. Allāh is Merciful and Kind. He disciplines us because He loves us and He wants the best for us.

Discipline is a way to correct mistakes and problems. When we do a good job, Allāh rewards us. When we do a bad job, Allāh corrects us by disciplining us.

Everyone needs discipline: Discipline is required everywhere. In a nice lawn, a weed is a bad plant. We need to remove the weed. If we do not remove the weed, the lawn will not look nice. In your class if a child disturbs teaching, he needs to be disciplined. The teacher may give him detention or send him to the principal. The purpose of discipline is to improve the quality of the class. Similarly, Allāh disciplines people when they go against Allāh and create trouble on earth.

Now and Hereafter: When people do bad things, they may be disciplined while on earth.[23:95] Sometimes they may be disciplined in the Hereafter.[78:22]

Many types of discipline: Sometimes a person does something bad and then feels guilty. The guilty feeling is a form of discipline from Allāh. Sometimes people are punished by Allāh to correct them. There were times when an entire community became bad. For example, many communities in the past refused to listen to their messengers. As a result, sometimes Allāh destroyed them. He destroyed the people of Nūh (A) with a flood.[7:64] He destroyed the people of Lūt (A) with an earthquake and a volcanic eruption.[11:82] As Nūh (A) and Lūt (A) were good people, they were saved along with their good followers.[54:13, 11:81] In lessons 21 and 22, we will learn about Hūd (A) and Sālih (A). We will see that Allāh disciplined the people of Hūd (A) and Sālih (A) when they did not listen to their prophets.

We should listen to Allāh: Allāh sends us warnings before He disciplines us.[41:4] The messengers told their people about Allāh's warnings.[54:18,23,30] The Qur'ān tells us that we will be disciplined if we do bad things. We should follow the teachings of the Qur'ān so that we are not punished.

If we think we are being disciplined for doing something bad, we should pray to Allāh to protect us. One such du'ā is:

$$\text{رَبِّ إِنِّى ظَلَمْتُ نَفْسِى فَاغْفِرْ لِى}$$

Rabbi innī zalamtu nafsī fa-ghfir lī.

My Rabb! I have indeed done harm to myself, therefore You protect me. (Al-Qasas 28:16)

Discipline or test: We cannot tell which event is discipline and which one is a test. Allāh says He will test all believers with fear, hunger, death, loss of earning, and so forth.[2:155] In another verse, Allāh says all believers will be tested, so that we know who is a better person.[29:2-3] Discipline and a test are not the same things.

Follow the teachings of the Nabi (S): We should follow the teachings of our Nabi Muhammad (S). We can find the best examples from his life and his activities. His examples are the **Sunnah**. Many of the sunnah are collected in the Hadīth. The Rasūl (S) did not do anything to oppose the Qur'ān.

Good Deeds

Bad Deeds

Allāh is Kind: Allāh disciplines us because He wants us to be good people. He disciplines us because He loves us and takes care of us. His discipline is never greater than the bad deed.[6:160] His reward is always greater than the good deed.[6:160]

Discipline by people: Allāh provides many types of discipline. In some cases, people may discipline other people who do bad things. Allāh told us how much discipline we may provide. Sometimes forgiveness is a good way to discipline others.[42:40]

1. Circle T if the sentence is true Circle F if the sentence is false.

Allāh disciplines us only on earth, not in the Hereafter. T F

Allāh disciplines us because He does not love us. T F

Allāh destroyed the people of Lūt (A) because they followed his teachings. T F

To avoid the discipline of Allāh, we should follow the Qur'ān. T F

2. One of the following choices is correct. Circle the correct choice.

   A. Allāh disciplines both good and bad people.
   B. Discipline and tests are the same things.
   C. Forgiveness is never a way to discipline.
   D. Allāh will strictly discipline us in Heaven.

3. Before disciplining us, what does Allāh do?

   _____

4. One of the following choices about the discipline of Allāh is correct. Circle the correct choice.

   A. Discipline is a way to encourage our mistakes.
   B. A large hurricane can be a form of discipline.
   C. When people refused to listen to the prophets, Allāh gave them rewards.
   D. Sometimes Shaitān disciplines us.

5. Memorize the du'ā, prayed by Mūsā (A). This du'ā is given in the lesson. Be prepared to recite the du'ā in front of your teacher in the next class.

Names of Allāh

Objective of the Lesson:

The most beautiful names belong to Allāh. These names tell us about Allāh's unique qualities. The more we learn about these qualities, the better we can understand Allāh. In this lesson, students will learn some names of Allāh and understand the significance of these names.

In the Qur'an, Allāh says the most beautiful names belong to Him.[7:180; 17:110] These names are beautiful because they express Allāh's qualities. These beautiful names of Allāh are called **al-Asmā al-husnā**. In the Qur'ān, Allāh mentions more than 99 of His names. All these names describe something good or special about Allāh.

In a famous Hadīth, Abu Hurairah, a companion of Rasūlullāh (S), narrated 99 names of Allāh. These names tell us the inner qualities of Allāh. Muslims learn the names of Allāh because the names carry countless blessings in them. We should try to learn as many of Allāh's names as we can, and then try to apply the beautiful qualities to our own behavior.

In the Qur'ān, Allāh mentioned the following about His names:

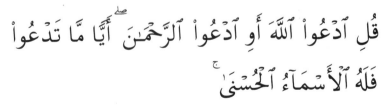

Say: "Call upon as Allāh or call upon as Rahman. By whatever you call, His are then the most beautiful names" (Bani Isra'il 17:110)

Today in this lesson, we will learn the first ten names of Allāh as described in the Hadīth. These ten names are **ar-Rahman, ar-Rahim, al-Malik, al-Quddus, as-Salam, al-Mu'min, al-Muhaimin, al-Azīz, al-Jabbar, and al-Mutakabbir.**

Ar-Rahman. The meaning of this name is most-Merciful, or most-Kind, or most-Beneficent. This name tells us that Allāh is full of mercy and kindness. He gives us everything in the world—air, water, weather, plants, grass, trees, daylight—everything is a gift. We do not do anything to earn these gifts. He gives these gifts on His own, without anybody asking for them. Even if we sin, Allāh still gives these things to us in this life.

Ar-Rahim. The meaning of this name is extremely loving and merciful. This name is very similar to Ar-Rahman. The name shows the quality of Allāh's special mercy both in this world and in the Hereafter. Allāh shows this special mercy as a result of our good deeds. The name ar-Rahman shows we get the mercy of Allāh even if we do not ask for it. The name ar-Rahim

shows we get this mercy based on our deeds. Whenever we do something good, we get rewards in this world and in the Hereafter.

Al-Malik. The meaning of this name is the Master or the King. Allāh is the Master of everything in the universe. He owns everything. He is more than a king. He is the King of all the kings.

Al-Quddus. The meaning of this name is the Holy, the Pure. This name tells us Allāh is the opposite of impure. He is above all evil or bad things. Since Allāh is pure, the name also indicates that He is perfect. There is no imperfection in Him.

As-Salam. This name means Allāh is the source of all Peace. All peace comes from Allāh.

Al-Mu'min. This name means the Guardian of faith. As Muslims, we believe there is no god but Allāh. We are the believers. Allāh is the Guardian of such believers and their faith in one Allāh.

Al-Muhaimin. This name means the Protector. Allāh protects us during every step in our lives.

Al-Azīz. The meaning of this name is the Mighty, the Strong.

Al-Jabbar. This name means one who pays off losses. When we experience a loss, Allāh recovers our loss. This name also indicates the power of Allāh.

Al-Mutakabbir. This name indicates that Allāh is the Majestic. Allāh is Grand and Noble. Nothing resembles Him, He is unlike anything that we see in other creatures.

Limitless Qualities of Allāh: Allāh's qualities, attributes, and essence are endless. We cannot fully describe the qualities of Allāh.[6:103] There is nothing that is similar to Him.[42:11] Allāh told us to pray to him by using these names.[7:180]

99 Beautiful Names of Allāh

Allāh	Allāh	As-Samiʿi	The Hearer of All
Ar-Rahman	The most-Kind	Al-Basīr	The Seer of All
Ar-Rahīm	The most-Rewarding	Al-Hakam	The Judge
Al-Malik	The Absolute Ruler	Al-ʿAdl	The Just
Al-Quddūs	The Pure One	Al-Latīf	The Subtle One
As-Salām	The Source of Peace	Al-Khabīr	The All-Aware
Al-Muʾmin	The Inspirer of Faith	Al-Halīm	The Forbearing
Al-Muhaymin	The Guardian	Al-ʿAzīm	The Magnificent
Al-ʿAzīz	The Victorious	Al-Ghafūr	The Forgiver
Al-Jabbār	The Compeller	Ash-Shakūr	The Appreciative
Al-Mutakabbīr	The Greatest	Al-ʿAli	The Highest
Al-Khāliq	The Creator	Al-Kabīr	The Greatest
Al-Bārīʾ	The Maker of Order	Al-Hafīz	The Preserver
Al-Musawwir	The Shaper of Beauty	Al-Muqīt	The Nourisher
Al-Ghaffār	The Forgiving	Al-Hasīb	The Accounter
Al-Qahhār	The Subduer	Al-Jalīl	The Mighty
Al-Wahhāb	The Giver of All	Al-Karīm	The Generous
Ar-Razzāq	The Sustainer	Ar-Raqīb	The Watchful One
Al-Fattāh	The Opener	Al-Mujīb	The Responder to Prayer
Al-ʿAlīm	The Knower of All	Al-Wāsīʿi	The All-Comprehending
Al-Qābid	The Constrictor	Al-Hakīm	The Perfectly Wise
Al-Bāsit	The Reliever	Al-Wadūd	The Loving One
Al-Khāfid	The Abaser	Al-Majīd	The Majestic One
Ar-Rāfiʿe	The Exalter	Al-Bāʿith	The Resurrector
Al-Muʿizz	The Bestower of Honors	Ash-Shahīd	The Witness
		Al-Haqq	The Truth
Al-Mudhill	The Humiliator	Al-Wakīl	The Trustee

Al-Qawi'	The Possessor of All Strength	Al-Wālī	The Protecting Friend
Al-Matīn	The Forceful One	Al-Muta'āli	The Supreme One
Al-Wali	The Governor	Al-Barr	The Doer of Good
Al-Hamīd	The Praised One	At-Tawwāb	The Guide to Repentance
Al-Muhsī	The Appraiser	Al-Muntaqim	The Avenger
Al-Mubdī'	The Originator	Al-'Afūw	The Forgiver
Al-Mu'īd	The Restorer	Ar-Ra'uf	The Clement
Al-Muhyī	The Giver of Life	Mālik al-Mulk	The Owner of All
Al-Mumīt	The Taker of Life	Dhul-Jalāli Wal-Ikrām	The Lord of Majesty
Al-Hayy	The Ever-Living One		
Al-Qayyum	The Self-Existing One	Al-Muqsīt	The Equitable One
Al-Wājid	The Finder	Al-Jāmi	The Gatherer
Al-Mājid	The Glorious	Al-Ghanī	The Rich One
Al-Wāhid	The Only One	Al-Mughnī	The Enricher
Al-Ahad	The One	Al-Māni'i	The Preventer of Harm
As-Samad	The Satisfier of All Needs	Ad-Dārr	The Creator of the Harmful
Al-Qādir	The All-Powerful		
Al-Muqtadir	The Creator of All Power	An-Nāfi'i	The Creator of Good
Al-Muqaddim	The Expediter	An-Nūr	The Light
Al-Mu'akhkhir	The Delayer	Al-Hādi	The Guide
Al-Awwal	The First	Al-Badī'	The Originator
Al-Akhir	The Last	Al-Bāqī	The Everlasting One
Az-Zāhir	The Manifest One	Al-Wārith	The Inheritor of All
Al-Bātin	The Hidden One	Ar-Rashīd	The Righteous Teacher
		As-Sabūr	The Patient One

Different versions of the 99 names include different names. Several other names are not included in the list. This indicates that Allāh actually has many more names. Below are a few names given as an example:

Al-Mu'tiy	The Bestower	Al-'Asim	The Protector
Al-Muhsin	The Giver	Al-Qasim	The One Who Shares
As-Sadiq	The True	Al-Muzakkī	The One Who Purifies
As-Sattar	The Veiler of Sin	As-Shafi'	The Intercessor
Ar-Rabb	The Sustainer/Cherisher	Al-Mudabbir	The Director
As-Sa'iq	The Driver to Hell	Al-Mawla	The Protector/Master
Al-Qareeb	The One Near		

1. What kinds of names belong to Allāh?

_____

2. What is the Arabic word for "most beautiful names"—a term used to describe all of Allāh's names?

    A.   Asma al-Allāh.
    B.   Asma al-Husna.
    C.   Asma al-Qur'ān.
    D.   Asma al-Rasul.

3. Read the first four verses of sūrah Fātiha in Arabic or its translation. Then count and write the beautiful names of Allāh that are mentioned in these four verses.

_____

4. Look at the list of 99 names of Allāh given in the chapter. From this list, identify three names that start with the following letters:

Starting with the letter "H": al-_____ , al-_____, al-_____

Starting with the letter "M": al-_____ , al-_____, al-_____

5. Read the meaning of the beautiful name ar-Rahman. Then write three things that Allāh gives us without any effort on our part.

    1) _____

    2) _____

    3) _____

Books of Allāh

Objective of the Lesson:

Allāh sent several divine books to people in the past. In this lesson, we will learn about these divine books. Who are the readers of the books? What is our understanding of these books? This lesson discusses the books of Allāh and provides a short overview of the books.

Allāh's greatest favor upon mankind is when He sent us guidance. If mankind had no guidance, we would have been totally lost and destroyed. Allāh sent guidance to mankind through **revealed books**. These are not ordinary books that people write. Revealed Books are those books that Allāh sent through angel Jibril to selected messengers. The revealed books contain the words of Allāh. These books are also called **Divine Books**. The word divine means anything that God sends.

Allāh says in the Qur'ān that He sent books to all the messengers.[6:89; 16:44; 35:25] Not all books were compiled and made into a formal book. For example, the divine guidance sent to prophet Ibrāhīm (A) was not collected in the form of a book. The Qur'ān says these were **suhuf,** or manuscripts.[87:19] Often divine guidance remained in people's memory for a while, but they did not write it down. After the prophets died, the divine guidance was slowly forgotten.

Four Books: The Qur'ān mentions the names of four revealed Books. These books are:

TORAH   PSALMS   GOSPEL

The Tawrāt was revealed to Mūsā (A), the Zabūr to Dāwūd (A), the Injīl to 'Isa (A), and the Qur'ān to Muhammad (S). The first three books were for small groups of people for a limited time. The Qur'ān is for all of mankind for all generations. Allāh protects the content of the Qur'ān from any kind of corruption.

Tawrāt	Revealed to Mūsā (A)	More than 3,000 years ago
Zabūr	Revealed to Dāwūd (A)	More than 2,900 years ago
Injīl	Revealed to 'Isa (A)	Around 32 C.E., about 1,970 years ago
Qur'ān	Revealed to Muhammad (S)	Between 610 C.E. and 632 C.E.

The Tawrāt: The original Tawrāt was revealed to Prophet Mūsā (A) more than three thousand years ago. It was revealed in the Hebrew language. It was a book of guidance to Bani Isra'il, or the Children of Israel. They were followers of Prophet Mūsā (A). The Tawrāt contained guidance, warning for bad deeds, clear explanations of many things, and the mercy of Allāh. The Qur'ān mentions the Tawrāt more than any other revealed book. The original copy of the revelation was lost during the course of history. However, the religious leaders of the Children of Israel memorized it and later wrote it down. When they wrote it down, they forgot to include certain parts of the revelation, and they added new parts that were not revealed by Allāh.

The Zabūr: The English name for Zabūr is **Psalms**. Today Psalms is included in the Bible. The present form of Psalms is not the original Zabūr revealed by Allāh. The books of Psalms contains songs to worship and celebrate the greatness of God. In Christian churches, people often sing passages from Psalms to glorify God.

The Injīl: The Injīl is the Arabic name for the revelation sent to prophet 'Isa (A). The meaning of the word Injīl is **Gospel**. Prophet 'Isa (A) came to confirm the original Tawrāt and he also brought new revelations of the Injīl. Therefore, the followers of 'Isa (A) read both the Tawrāt and the Injīl. Later the Christians included the Tawrāt, the Zabūr, and the Injīl in the Bible.

The Bible has two main parts: the **Old Testament** and the **New Testament**. The Old Testament includes the Tawrāt and the Zabūr.

The Injīl mentioned in the Qur'ān is not the same Bible read by Christians. Christians believe Injīl is the Gospel of the Bible. The Gospel of Christians is a compilation of several chapters, or individual books. These compilations were made hundred of years after 'Isa (A). The chapters, or books, inside the present-day Gospel were written by Christian saints based on the teachings of Jesus.

The Qur'ān: The Qur'ān is the final revealed Book of Allāh. The Qur'ān contains the words of Allāh exactly as they were revealed to our Rasūl Muhammad (S). Not a single word of the Qur'ān was changed, modified or deleted during the time of revelation or later. The Qur'ān was preserved from the very beginning of its revelation, both in written form and in the memory of the people. The position of the Qur'ān is above all the other revealed books of Allāh. It is the complete and perfect message sent by Allāh.

We may ask what would happen when a Christian or Jew adopts the Qur'ān. They would rediscover their faith in a correct and reliable form through the Qur'ān. The Qur'ān contains true and proper guidance for all people.

	**Points to Ponder**
	How are the texts of the Tawrāt, the Zabūr, and the Injīl different from the text of the Qur'ān?
	How are the chapters of the Injīl different from the chapters of the Qur'ān?

from**hadith**

It is narrated by 'Abdullah: When the following Verse was revealed: "It is those who believe and confuse not their belief with wrong" (6:83), the companions of Allāh's Apostle asked, "Who is amongst us who had not done injustice [wrong]?" Allāh revealed: "No doubt, joining others in worship with Allāh is a great injustice [wrong] indeed." (31.13) (Bukhārī)

1. Which divine book is the oldest in terms of when it was revealed?

    A.   Injīl.
    B.   Tawrāt.
    C.   Zabūr.
    D.   Qur'ān.

2. Approximately how many years ago was the original Tawrāt revealed?

_____

3. What happened to the original copy of the Tawrāt after its revelation?

_____

4. What are the two major parts of the present-day Bible?

_____

5. Tawrāt is included in one part of the Bible. What is the name of that part?

_____

6. Using an English translation of the Qur'an, read the last verse of Surah 68, *al-Qalam*. Is the message of the Qur'an for only a few people?

_____

Pre-Islamic Arabia: *Age of Ignorance*

Objective of the Lesson:

Before Islam came to Arabia, the people lived in ignorance. They had many false beliefs and senseless practices. Students will learn about the practices and beliefs of the people before Islam came to Arabia. This knowledge will help the students to understand why and how Islam changed the period of ignorance.

Before our Messenger Muhammad (S) preached Islam in Arabia, the condition of the people in Arabia was very different. The people practiced many bad things and believed in many false ideas. When Islam came to Arabia, it changed the social and religious conditions of the entire region. Islam changed all the bad practices and false beliefs. In this lesson, we will learn about pre-Islamic Arabia. Once we know about the false ideas during pre-Islamic Arabia, we can understand how Islam changed these false practices and ideas forever.

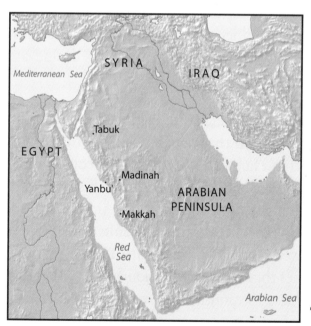

When we study Islam, we will often see a term called **Jāhiliyyah**. The word jāhiliyyah simply means "condition of ignorance."[33:33; 48:26] This term also means ignorance about the Islamic way of life and ignorance about divine guidance. Before the spread of Islam in Arabia, people had no knowledge of the Islamic way of life. Therefore, people were living in a condition of ignorance, or jāhiliyyah.

Islam changed the lives of the people in two major ways. The first change was what people believed. The second change was the way people behaved. These changes did not happen quickly. They took time and effort.

Religious beliefs of Arabs before Islam: Most pre-Islamic Arabs believed in and worshipped idols.[2:158] They believed each idol had the power to do certain things. They worshipped one idol for happiness, another for power, another for rainfall, another for children, and so on. At one time the Ka'bah was filled with more than three hundred idols.[17:81] Pre-Islamic Arabs believed that their gods could become angry and cause people to suffer, so they took special care of their idols. They had special ceremonies to keep the idols happy. For example, whenever they grew vegetables, crops or fruits, they brought a share for the idols.[6:137] When they slaughtered an animal, they brought some meat for the idols. Sometimes they slaughtered an animal in front of an idol to make the idol happy.[6:138] They knew the idols could not eat, so they let the priests of the temple take all the food brought to the temple.

Social beliefs of Arabs before Islam: Pre-Islamic Arabs believed in astrology and respected astrologers.[15:16–17; 37:7–10; 52:38, 41] **Astrology** is the false practice of predicting the future by looking at the stars. The movement and position of the stars have nothing to do with the future. Astrologers fool people by making them believe that whatever good or bad things happened in their lives was due to the movement of stars in the sky. The practice of foretelling the future was also common. Many fortune-tellers worshipped jinn or devils.

Drinking wine was common during the pre-Islamic period. During the Islamic period, people used to drink. However, Islam finally abolished the practice of drinking wine.

The people in Arabia were also **superstitious.**[2:189; 5:103; 6:137–141] Superstition is a false belief in unnatural things, magic, and false ideas about why certain things happen. Due to superstition, people used to set free some of their animals to honor their idols.[5:103] They would decide an important matter by shooting arrows. They would let some captive birds fly free, or observe the movement of other birds to decide an important matter.[7:131; 17:13]

Hajj before Muhammad (S): Pre-Islamic Arabs used to perform Hajj around the Ka'bah. Many of the things they did during Hajj were wrong. Some people would go around the Ka'bah naked. If the Hajj season did not fall during the right time of year, Arabs changed the date of Hajj to a better time that suited them.[9:36–37] Arabs followed a calendar year with twelve months, but sometimes they would add a month to the calendar in order to have 13 months in a year.

Position of women: During the pre-Islamic period, people did not like the birth of girls. They believed that the birth of daughters was evil or unlucky.[16:58-59; 43:17] Sometimes they would bury a newborn girl in the sand. They were happy only if a male child was born to their families. To them, the birth of a male child was a sign of tribal power.

Pre-Islamic Arabs did not like giving property to women and children. Women had no rights. They used to do many unfair things to women. For example, men married their own step-mothers in order to preserve the property.[4:22]

The rich and the poor: Rich people used to oppress the poor and powerless people. The rich would unfairly take the wealth of the orphans. If a man from one tribe killed a man from another tribe, the people of the second tribe took revenge in a very unfair way. They would not take revenge against the man who killed, but they would take revenge against the entire tribe. They would kill all the members of his tribe. As a result, ferocious fighting among tribes continued and bloodshed was common. People would not get justice—whoever had power was the winner.

Islam Brought Many Changes to Arabia

Some of the changes are:
- ✓ Stopped idolatry.
- ✓ Gave equal rights to women.
- ✓ Abolished burying infant girls.
- Granted inheritance rights to women.
- Stopped the practice of a man marrying his own step-mother.
- Stopped the practice of foretelling the future.
- Stopped the practice of astrology.
- Stopped the practice of setting food aside for divinity.
- ✓ Abolished drinking.
- Abolished false practices during Hajj.
- Stopped the practice of a man marrying two sisters at the same time.
- Discouraged all forms of superstition.
- Discouraged improper and excessive retaliation.

End of jāhiliyyah: The condition of jāhiliyyah did not last forever. After the Qur'ān was revealed, things began to change. It took 23 years to reveal the entire Qur'ān. Within this time, society changed, people changed and their belief system changed. As people began accepting Islam, they realized many things they practiced during jāhiliyyah did not make sense. Islam guided them towards the right path. Islam prohibited all of the jāhiliyyah practices. As people continued to change, they continued to see prosperity and improvement in their living standards. Arabia turned into a new nation, a new generation of people.

1. What is the simple meaning of the word jāhiliyyah?

_____

2. Mention two things people in Arabia used to BELIEVE during the period of jāhiliyyah.

1) _____

2) _____

3. Mention two things people in Arabia used to DO during the period of jāhiliyyah.

1) _____

2) _____

4. Write a short sentence about how people treated women during jāhiliyyah.

_____

5. When Islam came to Arabia, what happened to jāhiliyyah?

_____

6. During jāhiliyyah, people worshiped many gods. Using an English translation of the Qur'ān, read verse 51 of sūrah 16. What does Allāh tell us about worshipping two gods?

_____

The Year of the Elephant

Objective of the Lesson:

The year 570 C.E. is called the Year of the Elephant. Students will learn why the year was so named and what happened that year. Students will also learn about another important event that took place that year.

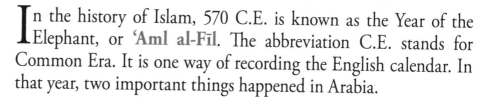

In the history of Islam, 570 C.E. is known as the Year of the Elephant, or **'Aml al-Fīl**. The abbreviation C.E. stands for Common Era. It is one way of recording the English calendar. In that year, two important things happened in Arabia.

Long before the religion of Islam was established, Makkah was an important city in Arabia. The city was established when Ibrāhīm (A) settled his family there. Later he built the Ka'bah with his son Ismā'īl (A). He prayed to Allāh to make the city safe and provide its people with food.[2:126] Allāh asked Ibrāhīm (A) to declare Hajj. People came to the city from every remote part of the world.[22:27] In the course of time, the main attraction in Makkah became the annual Hajj and the Ka'bah.

Every year thousands of people came to Makkah for Hajj. During the time of Hajj, local people had good business. They prepared and sold food for thousands of people and gave them places to sleep. People brought different products with them and sold them in the market. Makkah became a rich city.

Abrahah's anger: The ruler of **Yemen** was a Christian man named **Abrahah**. He was jealous that the city of Makkah was richer than his city in Yemen. Makkah was a rich city because a large number of pilgrims came there every year. Abrahah wanted to attract the pilgrims to his city and profit from trade activities. He built a large church in Yemen, hoping that many pilgrims would come there every year. Even after a few years, he did not see pilgrims or make money. The church had no history, whereas the Ka'bah had a long history dating back to Ibrāhīm (A). People respected Ibrāhīm (A) and believed the pilgrimage to the Ka'bah was good for them.

Abrahah was furious. He realized that as long as the Ka'bah existed, people would not come to Yemen. He decided to destroy the Ka'bah. He thought that if the Ka'bah was destroyed, people would have no other choice but to go to Yemen for the pilgrimage.

Abrahah comes towards Makkah: In order to destroy the Ka'bah, Abrahah marched towards Makkah with a large army. His army included African elephants. He brought the elephants to demolish the Ka'bah to the ground. After arriving near Makkah, he camped a few miles outside the city. He sent his soldiers to announce his arrival to the Quraish. The soldiers captured many camels of the Quraish in order to make it difficult for them to fight. Many of the camels belonged to **Abdul Muttalib**, the leader of the Quraish and the grandfather of Muhammad (S).

Abdul Muttalib went to Abrahah to demand the return of his camels. Abrahah thought Abdul Muttalib came with a request not to destroy the Ka'bah. He asked Abdul Muttalib why he was worried about the camels but not the Ka'bah. Abdul Muttalib replied that he was the master of the camels, therefore he worried about them. The Ka'bah has a Master too, who would take care of it. Abdul Muttalib meant that Allāh would protect the Ka'bah.

> **Interesting Facts**
>
> African elephants are different from Asian elephants. Many people know about the larger ears of the African elephants. Here are a few more differences:
>
> African elephants have four nails on the front feet, while Asian elephants have five. On the back feet, African elephants have three nails, and Asian elephants have four.
>
> Asian female elephants have no tusks, but some males have tusks. All African male and many female elephants have tusks.

The Quraish realized they were too weak to resist the mighty forces of Abrahah. They left the city and took shelter in the adjoining hills. Abdul Muttalib also left the city. Before leaving the city, he prayed to Allāh to protect the Ka'bah.

Allāh protected the Ka'bah: With no one to defend the Ka'bah, it became an easy target for Abrahah. At that time, something strange happened. Some kind of disease spread among the troops before they could destroy the Ka'bah. The troops became confused.[105:2] Then Allāh sent a large number of birds over them.[105:3] It is reported that the birds pelted rocks upon them and the entire army became disoriented. Very soon the troops began to die. This incident is mentioned in **sūrah al-Fīl**.

Abrahah came to destroy the Ka'bah, but he was defeated without fighting any battle. Allāh protected the Ka'bah from destruction. The people of Arabia wrote poems and sang songs about this incident for a long time. Historians later named the year 570 C.E. as the **Year of the Elephant**, or **'Aml al-Fīl**.

An event that begins a civilization: Another important event happened a few months after Abrahah invaded Makkah. Abdul Muttalib, the Quraish leader, was blessed with a grandson. The father of the baby boy was 'Abdullah, and his mother was Aminah. The birth of the baby was an emotional event for Abdul Muttalib because 'Abdullah died a few months before the birth of the baby boy. This baby boy was none other than our beloved Nabi Muhammad (S).

Sūrah al-Fīl

With the name of Allāh, most Gracious, most Rewarding.

سُوْرَةُ الْفِيْلِ

بِسْمِ اللهِ الرَّحْمٰنِ الرَّحِيْمِ

أَلَمْ تَرَ كَيْفَ فَعَلَ رَبُّكَ بِأَصْحٰبِ الْفِيْلِ ۝

Have you not seen how your Lord dealt with the fellows of the Elephant?

أَلَمْ يَجْعَلْ كَيْدَهُمْ فِيْ تَضْلِيْلٍ ۝

Did He not turn their plot into confusion?

وَأَرْسَلَ عَلَيْهِمْ طَيْرًا أَبَابِيْلَ ۝

And He sent against them flocks of birds,

تَرْمِيْهِمْ بِحِجَارَةٍ مِّنْ سِجِّيْلٍ ۝

Casting them against stones of baked clay;

فَجَعَلَهُمْ كَعَصْفٍ مَّأْكُوْلٍ ۝

So He made them like straw eaten up.

Note: C.E. stands for Common Era. The numbering of the year is identical to the A.D. system. Common Era is preferred because it does not have any religious titles referring to Jesus Christ.

1. How many important events happened in Arabia in the Year of the Elephant?

    A.   One important event.
    B.   Two important events.
    C.   Five important events.
    D.   Seven important events.

2. Which of the following choices best explains the reason Abrahah built a church in Yemen?

    A.   There was no church in Yemen.
    B.   He wanted to help the people.
    C.   He wanted to attract pilgrims to Yemen.
    D.   He wanted to bring elephants to the Ka'bah.

3. When Abrahah marched to Makkah with a large army and elephants, how did the Quraish react?

_____

4. How did the gathering of a large number of pilgrims benefit the people of Makkah?

_____

5. Why did the pilgrims not like to go to Yemen, even though Abrahah built a large church?

    A.   Yemen was too far.
    B.   Yemen was a dangerous place.
    C.   People in Yemen were unfriendly.
    D.   The church did not have a history, but the Ka'bah had a long history.

6. Circle T if the statement is true. Circle F if the statement is false.

When the army of Abrahah arrived, the Quraish welcomed them.	T	F
Some kind of disease spread and the birds pelted rocks at the army.	T	F
The elephants destroyed the Ka'bah, but Abdul Muttalib rebuilt it.	T	F
The Year of the Elephant is also known as 'Aml al-Hajj.	T	F
Muhammad (S) was born a few months after the attack by Abrahah.	T	F

Early Life of Muhammad (S)

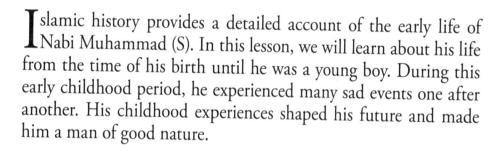

Objective of the Lesson:

Students will learn about the early life of Muhammad (S) from the time of his birth until he was a youth. This lesson provides an overview of twists and turns in Rasulūllāh's life. Much of what happened later in his life was shaped by his experiences during childhood.

Islamic history provides a detailed account of the early life of Nabi Muhammad (S). In this lesson, we will learn about his life from the time of his birth until he was a young boy. During this early childhood period, he experienced many sad events one after another. His childhood experiences shaped his future and made him a man of good nature.

Muhammad (S) was born in 570 C.E., the same year Abrahah attacked Makkah with a troop of elephants. Rasūlullāh's (S) father was Abdullah and his mother was Aminah. His grandfather was Abdul Muttalib. Before Muhammad (S) was born, his father died while returning from a trip to Syria.

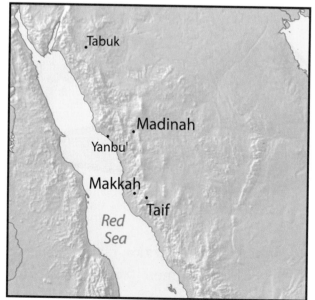

Nurse-mother Halīmah: It was the custom at that time to place all newborn babies under the care of a nurse-mother. After two or three years, the babies were returned to their birth mothers. Usually the nurse-mothers were poor women. They earned good money by taking care of the infants.

In the year Muhammad (S) was born, several babies were born in Makkah to many families.

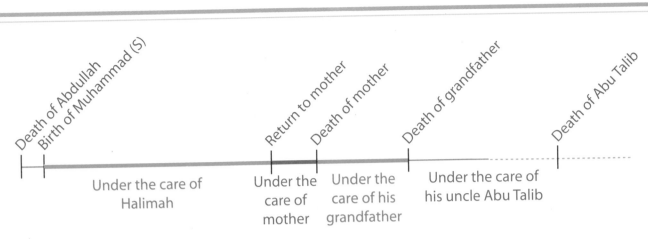

Death of Abdullah
Birth of Muhammad (S)

Return to mother

Death of mother

Death of grandfather

Death of Abu Talib

Under the care of Halimah

Under the care of mother

Under the care of his grandfather

Under the care of his uncle Abu Talib

Nurse-mothers from nearby places came to Makkah, hoping to find babies to take care of from wealthy families. Many nurse-mothers did not consider taking care of Muhammad (S) because his father was dead. His mother was not rich. A nurse-mother named **Halīmah** could not find a baby from a wealthy family, so she took infant Muhammad (S) under her care. She knew that the baby's father had died and the family might not pay her well. But she did not want to return home empty-handed.

Halīmah returned to her tribe in the village of **Tā'if** with infant Muhammad (S). Within a few days, she started noticing changes in her family. Somehow the family began receiving all kinds of blessings. Their goats started giving enough milk, the goats gave birth to more babies, and the food that used to last for two days now started lasting for four days. The family began to experience happiness and comfort. Everything they did appeared to be a blessing. Earlier she wanted a baby from a wealthy family as a source of income to maintain her family. But now with infant Muhammad (S) in their family, things were much better. Halīmah did not know why things were getting better, but she felt it was due to the baby. She knew the baby brought them good fortune. Her family knew the baby had something special in him.

A short stay with Mother Aminah: Two years later when Muhammad (S) was a toddler, Halīmah brought him back to his mother Aminah. At that time, people in Makkah were suffering from widespread disease. Aminah did not want Muhammad (S) to get the disease. Therefore, she sent him back with Halīmah to protect him from the bad air of Makkah. Besides, Halīmah herself wanted to keep the lovely toddler Muhammad (S) with her for a few more years.

Mother Aminah passes away: Muhammad (S) remained under the care of Halīmah until the age of five. After he returned to his mother, Aminah, he lived with her for about a year. When he was a little over six years old, his mother passed away.

Before the death of his mother, Muhammad (S) was already a half-orphan because his father had passed away. Now, after the death of his mother, he became an orphan—without both of his parents. At that time his grandfather, Abdul Muttalib, became his guardian. Abdul Muttalib was a very old man. He was too weak to take care of a young boy, but he did not hesitate.

The loving grandfather: Muhammad (S) received good care from his old grandfather, who loved him very much. Abdul Muttalib was a Quraish leader. Young Muhammad (S) went to many meetings of the tribal chiefs with his grandfather. He listened to the chiefs talk. He learned many important things from their discussions. He did not have a chance to live with his grandfather for very long. When Muhammad (S) was about eight years old, his grandfather passed away. Once again, Muhammad (S) was without a guardian. One sad event came after another. By the age of eight, young Muhammad (S) experienced three deaths: his father, his mother, and then his grandfather.

Under the care of an uncle: After the death of his grandfather, his uncle **Abū Tālib** took responsibility for taking care of him. Abū Tālib was not a wealthy man. He had difficulty in maintaining his own family. Yet, he could not let young Muhammad (S) grow up without a guardian. Muhammad (S) had other uncles who could have taken care of him, but Abū Tālib came forward because he loved the young boy very much. It was Allāh's plan to place Muhammad (S) under the care of Abū Tālib. He was a Quraish leader. When Muhammad (S) would later become the messenger of Allāh, Abū Tālib protected him from the anger of the Quraish. Nobody dared to harm Muhammad (S) because he was under the care of Abū Tālib.

1. What was the name of the nurse-mother who took care of Muhammad (S) when he was a newborn baby?

_____

2. What special things began to happen in the nurse-mother's house when infant Muhammad (S) went to live with them?

_____

_____

3. After Halīmah brought Muhammad (S) to Aminah, why was Muhammad (S) returned to stay with Halīmah for a few more years?

_____

_____

4. How old was Muhammad (S) when his grandfather died?

_____

5. Circle T if the sentence is true. Circle F if the sentence is false.

Muhammad (S) spent about ten years with his nurse-mother Halīmah.　　T　F

After Aminah died, Abu Tālib became the first guardian of Muhammad (S) for a few years.　　T　F

Muhammad (S) remained under the care of Abū Talib for two years.　　T　F

Life Before Becoming a Nabi

Objective of the Lesson:

Before Muhammad (S) became a nabi or messenger of Allāh, he demonstrated many positive qualities in his conduct and dealings. This lesson describes some of the key events that influenced the future of Rasūlullāh (S).

Muhammad (S) became a nabi or a messenger of Allāh when he was 40 years old. In this lesson, we will learn about Muhammad's (S) life since his childhood until he became a nabi. Many important things happened in his life during this period.

In the previous lesson, we learned that when Muhammad (S) was about eight years old, his grandfather passed away. At that time, his uncle, Abū Tālib, took responsibility for looking after him.

Abū Tālib was a Quraish leader and a merchant. He often traveled to Syria and Yemen to trade. On one of his trips to Syria, Abu Tālib took his nephew, Muhammad (S), with him. In Syria they met a Christian monk named **Bahirah**. This man knew many things about religion. He read from ancient books that a nabi would come to Arabia. When he saw young Muhammad (S), he recognized that the boy would be a nabi one day. He told Abū Tālib to take good care of the boy because he was special.

In Makkah everybody loved young Muhammad (S) because of his good nature and sincerity. People lovingly called him **Al-Amin,** the trustworthy, and **As-Sadiq,** the truthful. This was because Muhammad (S) never told lies.

Family life of Rasūlullāh (S): When Muhammad (S) was a young man, a rich widow named **Khadījah** hired him to conduct business on her behalf. She sent him to Syria to trade. After he returned from Syria and handed over the entire profit from the trade, Khadījah was deeply impressed. She asked Muhammad (S) to marry her. At that time, Muhammad (S) was 25 years old and Khadījah was 40 years old. They were married and had several children. All of their sons died during childhood or earlier, but all of their daughters survived. Their dearest daughter was Fātimah.

Nabi Muhammad (S) lived in a society where sons were preferred by everybody and new-born daughters were often buried alive. But not in the family of Nabi Muhammad (S). All the daughters received loving care in the family. There was a young slave in their family. His name was **Zaid Ibn Harith.** Khadījah had given Zaid as a gift to Nabi Muhammad (S). Later Nabi Muhammad (S) adopted Zaid as his son.

Solving a problem: When Muhammad (S) was about 25 years old, the Quraish decided to rebuild the Ka'bah. The foundation of the Ka'bah was damaged due to a recent flood. All the clans under the Quraish tribe helped reconstruct the Ka'bah. A problem arose when

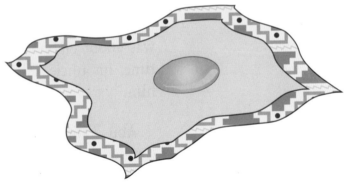

the famous **Black Stone** was ready to be placed in its right place on the east wall. Each clan wanted the honor of placing the Black Stone. They argued about it but a conclusion was not reached. The clans were almost on the verge of fighting with each other on this issue. Ultimately, they agreed to listen to Muhammad's (S) decision because they trusted him. He solved the problem in a unique way. He took a sheet of cloth and spread it on the ground. Then he placed the Black Stone on the cloth. He told each member of the clan to hold the cloth, lift it, and carry the Black Stone to the east wall of the Ka'bah. Thus, no single person or clan carried the stone, but everyone carried it together. The problem was solved in a friendly manner. People liked Muhammad's (S) decision.

Social problems: Muhammad (S) felt very bad when he saw that the people in Makkah were greedy, corrupt, and ignorant. He disliked how people treated the poor and women. He thought that if something good did not happen to the community, they would be ruined. He realized that the spiritual condition of the people in Makkah was very bad. The idols they worshipped were mere stones—they could not speak, think, or help. These idols could not bring truth, let alone happiness, into people's lives.

Muhammad (S) wanted to find truth, but he realized truth could not be found in the words of rabbis, Christian monks or other religious people who gathered at the time of Hajj. He wondered who created the sun, the moon, and the stars. He wondered who brought the rain and who provided the air. People live and die, but why were they born and what was the purpose of life? Sometimes he wondered if he was going insane from all these thoughts.

Cave Hira: Muhammad (S) particularly loved to go to a cave named **Hira** in a mountain near Makkah. The mountain and the cave were a few miles northeast of Makkah. Every year in the month of Ramadan, he went to the cave and spent a long time there. In the quietness inside the cave, Muhammad (S) was able to concentrate and reach a new level of thinking.

One day when he was about 40 years old, he was meditating in Cave Hira. At that time, angel Jibril (A) appeared before him. The angel brought divine revelation. Muhammad (S) was selected to become a messenger of Allāh.

Points To Ponder
Before becoming a messenger of Allāh, what were some of the ways Muhammad (S) proved that he was a man with superior talent?
People had idol gods all over Makkah, but why was Muhammad (S) not happy with these idol gods?

1. What was the name of the Christian monk who said Muhammad (S) would be a messenger one day?

    A.   Abrahah.
    B.   Abdul Muttalib.
    C.   Bahirah.
    D.   Halīmah.

2. How did Muhammad (S) solve the dispute about placing the Black Stone after the Ka'bah was repaired?

_____

_____

_____

3. Circle T if the sentence is true, circle F if the sentence is false.

People lovingly called Muhammad (S) Al-Amin or As-Sadiq.   T   F

Muhammad (S) loved to spend quiet time in Cave Hira and seek truth.   T   F

Cave Hira is located two miles north of Madinah.   T   F

When Muhammad (S) married Khadījah (ra), she was 40 years old.   T   F

4. What was the name of the slave whom Muhammad (S) adopted as his son?

_____

5. Where did Muhammad (S) receive the first divine revelation?

    A.   At the east wall of the Ka'bah.
    B.   In his home when he was sleeping.
    C.   In Cave Hira.
    D.   In Syria when he met a monk.

First Revelation

Objective of the Lesson:

The history of how Muhammad (S) received the first divine revelation is fascinating. Students will learn about the events in Cave Hira and the first verses of the revelation. Students will also learn about how a terrified Muhammad (S) reacted and how his wife, Khadījah, helped him.

Muhammad (S) received the first revelation when he was 40 years old. Islamic history has reported in detail about the incident when he received the words of Allāh. It was a unique experience for him. Let us learn more about how and where he received God's word.

Muhammad's (S) life before revelation: In the previous two lessons, we studied Muhammad's (S) life during his childhood and adult life. After his marriage with Khadījah (ra) and success in business, his family lived in comfort. During this period, Muhammad (S) was deeply disturbed by the moral and spiritual condition of people in Makkah. He was unhappy about how the rich treated the poor. He was unhappy about people worshipping idols that could not help anybody. He felt these idols could not be god. He would often go to a quiet place to think about the purpose of life and who could be God of the whole world.

Quiet time in Cave Hira: Every year the good and spiritual minded people in Makkah went to quiet places to meditate. Muhammad (S) was a good person. His conduct was excellent and he was trusted by everybody as a person who never spoke a lie. Every year Muhammad (S) went to a lonely, quiet place to think about life and God.

Cave Hira was located slightly outside of Makkah. When Muhammad (S) learned about a cave in the mountain, he decided to spend time there. Every year during the month of Ramadan, he began to go to the cave and spend hours and sometimes days in the cave. His main purpose was to find the Truth. He knew the idols that people worshipped were not the true God. He wanted to find out the purpose of life. Was it just to live and die? What happens to people after they die?

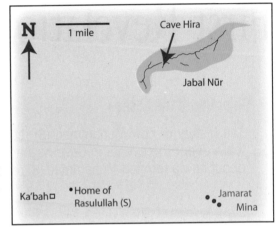

Receipt of divine message: In 610 C.E. when Ramadan began, Muhammad (S) spent time in Cave Hira in Jabal Nūr. He was 40 years old. During one of the last ten nights of that Ramadan, a strange thing happened to Muhammad (S). While meditating in the cave, suddenly he heard a voice command him to read. The actual Arabic word was "**Iqrā**," which means "You read!" or simply "Read!" It was a strange feeling. He could not see who was speaking to him. He replied, "I do not know how to read." Then Muhammad (S) felt his entire body being squeezed and getting crushed. When he felt relief, again he heard the voice telling him to read. Again he replied that he did not know how to read. Then he felt himself being squeezed so tightly that he nearly suffocated. Then he relaxed, and the feeling of being squeezed was gone. Again for the third time, he heard the voice say, "Read! In the name of your Rabb who created . . ."

Then a change came over him. He was able to repeat the words after they were recited to him. It was angel Jibril who came to deliver Allāh's message. Angel Jibril recited five verses and Muhammad (S) repeated the words after him.

اقْرَأْ بِاسْمِ رَبِّكَ الَّذِى خَلَقَ ۞

1. Read in the name of your Rabb who created

خَلَقَ الْإِنسَـٰنَ مِنْ عَلَقٍ ۞

2. He has created man from a clot

اقْرَأْ وَرَبُّكَ الْأَكْرَمُ ۞

3. Read and your Rabb is the most Gracious

الَّذِى عَلَّمَ بِالْقَلَمِ ۞

4. Who has taught by the pen

عَلَّمَ الْإِنسَـٰنَ مَا لَمْ يَعْلَمْ ۞

5. He has taught man that which he did not know

The five ayat: The five ayat, or verses were the first revealed verses of the Qur'ān. With these verses, the revelation of the Qur'ān began. Muhammad (S) was now a nabi or messenger of Allāh. These first five verses were later compiled in the Qur'ān in Sūrah 96, **Sūrah al-'Alaq.**

Frightening experience: The cave itself was dark and lonely. Most people would be scared in the cave. The initial experience with angel Jibril scared Muhammad (S). It was natural to be scared, as he had never experienced such an event before. At first he thought some evil spirit or jinn had overpowered him. In the past, on many occasions, he saw how some of the Arab poets experienced spells over their bodies that they claimed were caused by jinn. Muhammad (S) was not sure, but he was very scared.

Khadījah (ra) comforts him: Muhammad (S) returned home quickly, shivering in fear and anxiety. He was very disturbed. When he reached home, he repeatedly asked his wife, Khadījah (ra), to wrap him with a blanket. After a while when he calmed down, he explained everything to her. She assured him that this experience could not be due to an evil spirit. She assured him that Allāh would never let him down because he was so kind to the poor and good to people.

Interesting Facts
The home of Rasulullah (S) was about 1,030 feet above sea level and a few hundred yards from the Ka'bah.
The peak of Jabal Nūr, where Cave Hira is located, is about 1,770 feet above sea level. It is a few miles northeast of Ka'bah.

Waraqah explains the incident: Later Khadījah (ra) took Muhammad (S) to her cousin **Waraqah ibn Naufal.** Her cousin was a Christian. He was also a knowledgeable person. He listened to the incident carefully. Then he explained that it must be the same angel Jibril who had come to prophet Mūsā. Angel Jibril had now come to Muhammad (S). Waraqah assured him that angel Jibril would not come unless he had a mission. That mission was to bring divine revelation.

1. Circle T if the sentence is true. Circle F if it is false.

A.	Waraqah was Khadījah's uncle.	T	F
B.	The first verses of the Qur'ān came during Ramadan.	T	F
C.	Cave Hira is slightly outside Madinah.	T	F
D.	Angel Jibril went to Cave Hira to deliver divine message.	T	F

2. At what age did Muhammad (S) receive the first revelation?

  A. Age 25.
  B. Age 40.
  C. Age 23.
  D. Age 50.

3. How many verses were revealed at the first revelation in Cave Hira?

_____

4. When was the first set of revelations sent to Muhammad (S)?

  A. During the first 10 days of Dhul Hajj.
  B. During the last 10 days of Muharram.
  C. During the last 10 days of Shawwal.
  D. During the last 10 days of Ramadan.

5. After Muhammad (S) came back from Cave Hira, Khadījah (ra) took him to her cousin. Who was the cousin and what did he tell them?

_____

_____

6. Which sūrah contains the first set of revelations?

_____

Makkan Period: *The Early Years of the Muslims*

Objective of the Lesson:

This lesson provides a short summary of the entire Makkan period of Islam, starting from the time Muhammad (S) received the first revelation until he planned to migrate to Madīnah.

We have already learned about the early life of our Nabi Muhammad (S). Today we will learn a brief history of his life in Makkah. This time of his life is known as the Makkan Period. The time of his life spent in Madīnah is known as the Madinan Period. During both time periods, many important things happened in his life and in the history of Islam.

Muhammad (S) was born in Makkah. His father was Abdullah and his mother was Amina.

As a little boy, Muhammad (S) lived in a village called Tā'if with a nurse-mother named **Halīmah**. When he was five, Muhammad (S) came back to his mother. When Muhammad (S) was six years old, his mother passed away. His grandfather, **Abdul Muttalib**, took care of him. A few years later, his grandfather passed away, too. Young Muhammad (S) was now with a very caring uncle, **Abū Tālib**.

Trips to faraway lands: Abū Tālib once took Muhammad (S) with him on a long trade journey. People at that time traveled on animal backs or on foot. When Muhammad (S) was older, he worked for other people. He bought and sold things for other people. He also worked for his wife, **Khadījah**, who was a rich business woman.

New Muslims: When Rasulullah (S) became a nabi, or messenger, not many people listened to him. In the first few years, only a few people became Muslim. Other people of Makkah, who used to worship idols, did not like the religion of Islam. They were not ready to give up their idols and worship One Allah. They were mean to Rasulullah (S) and to other Muslims. The new Muslims had to pray in hiding. Abū Tālib was a powerful leader, and he protected Muhammad (S) from bad people.

Difficult times: Within the first five years after Muhammad (S) became the messenger of Allāh, the situation turned bad for the Muslims. The idol-worshippers continued to torture the Muslims. At one point, Rasūlullāh (S) told many of his followers to leave Makkah and move to **Abyssinia**. It is a place in East Africa in Ethiopia. The ruler of Abyssinia was a Christian. He protected the Muslims and allowed them to live in his country.

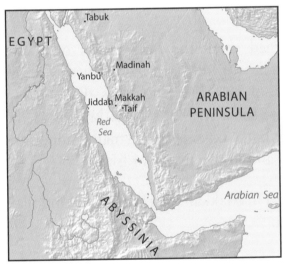

During these difficult times, uncle Abū Tālib passed away. Within a short time, Khadījah (ra) also passed away. According to tribal norms, an elderly powerful man guards or protects others. For a short time, **Abū Lahab**, an uncle of Rasūlullāh (S), became his guardian. But quickly, Abū Lahab refused to protect him because he did not like what Nabi Muhammad (S) taught. Abū Lahab became very mean to Rasūlullāh (S) and the Muslims. The people in Makkah became violent towards the Muslims.

In order to be safe, some Muslims were already in Abyssinia. Those who were in Makkah also needed safety. Rasūlullāh (S) went to **Tā'if**, where he grew up as a child. He hoped that the people of Tā'if would listen to his message and provide protection to the Muslims. The elders of Tā'if did not like Muhammad (S). They asked people of Tā'if to chase him out of the city. Rasūlullāh (S) was injured. He came back to Makkah without success.

Pledge of 'Aqabah: During the last two years of Rasūlullāh's (S) life in Makkah, a group of people from a city called **Yathrib** came to Makkah. They met with Nabi Muhammad (S) and invited him to settle in Yathrib. These people made two pledges with Rasūlullāh (S). A pledge is a promise or agreement to do something. These pledges became known as the **Pledges of 'Aqabah**. We will study the pledges in detail in the next lesson. Due to these pledges, Muhammad (S) was finally able to move to Yathrib. Later this city became known as Madīnah.

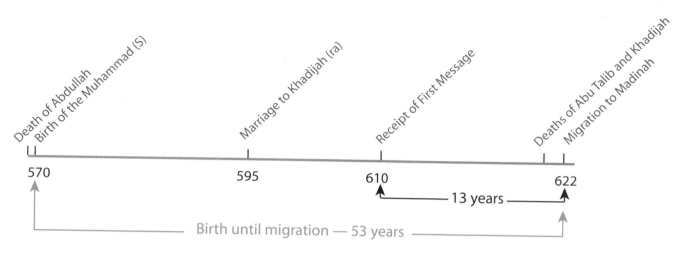

Time line of Rasūlullāh's (S) early life in Makkah

Plot to kill Muhammad (S): The powerful people in Makkah were angry with the progress of Islam. They did not like Muhammad (S) or his followers to speak against their idols. They did not like the way Muhammad (S) tried to end of many false practices of the non-believers in Makkah.

During the last year of his life in Makkah, the non-believers in Makkah decided to kill Muhammad (S). One night they assembled in front of his house to kill him. But Rasūlullāh (S) was able to escape. In another chapter we will study in detail how he escaped and what happened next. Rasūlullāh (S) then migrated to Yathrib that was later named as Madīnah. This migration is called **hijrah**. From the time Muhammad (S) became a messenger until he migrated to Madīnah, he lived in Makkah for 13 years.

Muslims were now much safer in Madinah than they were in Makkah.

	**Points to Ponder**
	What were some of the ways the Quraish made life difficult for Nabi Muhammad (S)?
	When Rasūlullāh (S) faced difficult conditions in Makkah, instead of giving up, what were some of the steps he took to overcome the difficulties?

1. Name the village where Muhammad (S) lived as a child with his nurse-mother Halima.

    _____

2. Four people took care of, or became guardians of, young Muhammad (S). Name them in order since his birth.

    1) _____
    2) _____
    3) _____
    4) _____

3. During difficult times in Makkah, where did some of the Muslims migrate?

    A. Syria.
    B. Egypt.
    C. Abyssinia.
    D. Morocco.

4. People from Yathrib came to Makkah and made two pledges. What were the names of the pledges?

    A. Pledges of Makkah.
    B. Pledges of Hudaibiyah.
    C. Pledges of Tā'if.
    D. Pledges of Aqabah.

5. After Muhammad (S) became a messenger and until he migrated to Madīnah, how long did he live in Makkah?

    A. 5 years.
    B. 10 years.
    C. 13 years.
    D. 32 years.

Pledges of 'Aqabah: *Invitation to Migrate*

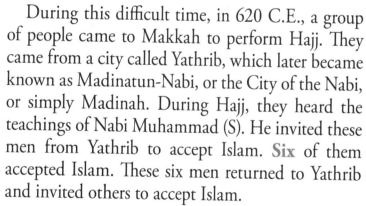

Objective of the Lesson:

Rasūlullāh's (S) migration to Madīnah was made possible by two pledges that came to be known as the Pledges of Aqabah. Who were these people and why did they make the pledges? Students will learn about these events and their significance in shaping the history of Islam.

After becoming the messenger of Allāh, Muhammad (S) lived in Makkah for 13 years. He received the first revelation in 610 C.E. Nine years after he received the first revelation, his uncle Abū Tālib and wife Khadījah (ra) passed away. Our Nabi Muhammad's (S) life was already difficult, but after the deaths of his wife and uncle, his life became even more difficult. People in Makkah respected him as a good man, but most of them did not like his teachings. These non-believers were planning to harm him.

During this difficult time, in 620 C.E., a group of people came to Makkah to perform Hajj. They came from a city called Yathrib, which later became known as Madinatun-Nabi, or the City of the Nabi, or simply Madinah. During Hajj, they heard the teachings of Nabi Muhammad (S). He invited these men from Yathrib to accept Islam. **Six** of them accepted Islam. These six men returned to Yathrib and invited others to accept Islam.

The first pledge: In 621 C.E., **12** people came from Yathrib to perform Hajj. They met with Rasūlullāh (S) in a place called **al-'Aqabah**, near Makkah, and made an agreement with him. In the history of Islam, this agreement is known as the **First Pledge of al-'Aqabah**. A pledge is a promise or agreement to do something. Rasūlullāh (S) asked them to make several oaths. Some of the main oaths were:

- To obey none but Allāh
- Not to steal
- Not to kill their children
- Not to commit any evil

Rasūlullāh (S) told them that if they followed the oath, Allāh would be happy with them. Allāh would reward them with a life in Heaven. These people went back to Yathrib and told others about Islam. Through them even more people accepted Islam.

The second pledge: The following year, in 622 C.E., **75** people came from Yathrib to Makkah to perform Hajj. Among them were two women. During Hajj, they had another secret meeting with Rasūlullāh (S) in al-'Aqabah. This time they took another oath. This oath is known in the history of Islam as the **Second Pledge of al-'Aqabah**. This oath was similar to the first oath, but it was more detailed.

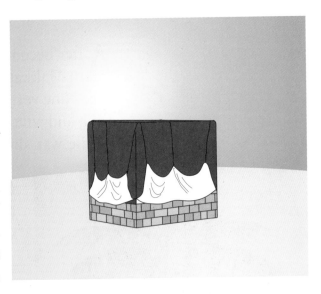

During these secret meetings, the people of Yathrib learned that Nabi Muhammad's (S) life in Makkah was becoming very difficult. They learned that most of the Makkans did not like Islam. They also learned that the top leaders in Makkah opposed Muhammad (S) or his teachings. These leaders were planning to stop Rasūlullāh (S) from teaching Islam. They were even ready to kill him to stop him.

An invitation to move: These 75 Muslims from Yathrib invited Nabi Muhammad (S) to come to Yathrib, live with them and continue his preaching. **Al-'Abbās**, one of Rasūlullāh's (S) uncles, was present during the secret meeting. He was not yet a Muslim, but he loved his nephew. He was concerned for his nephew just as the people from Yathrib were concerned. He explained to the people of Yathrib the danger of having Nabi Muhammad (S) among them. He told them that the Makkans would not like it and that they might take revenge on the people of Yathrib. He also advised them that if they really wanted Nabi Muhammad (S) to go with them, they had to protect him at all costs. All the 75 people from Yathrib promised to protect Muhammad (S). This was the main point in the Second Pledge of al-'Aqabah.

The people from Yathrib promised to lead a good life and protect Nabi Muhammad (S) as they would protect their own women and children. They declared that it would be a duty upon them to protect Muhammad (S) if anyone from Makkah attacked them.

At the end of Hajj and after taking the Pledge of al-'Aqabah, these 75 people left. Rasūlullāh (S) stayed in Makkah, waiting for the best opportunity to leave the city. When the Makkans learned about the pledge, they became angry. They went to Yathrib and asked the people to cancel the pledges, but the people of Yathrib refused.

Evil plans of the Makkans: The Makkans returned home and began serious discussions about what to do with Muhammad (S). They realized that if Muhammad (S) went to Yathrib, he might convert the entire city to Islam and create problems for the Makkans. Finally, the idol-worshippers of Makkah decided to kill him. One night, several men from the Quraish tribe gathered outside Rasūlullāh's (S) home to kill him. However, late in the night, Rasūlullāh (S) secretly left his house. 'Ali, Rasulullah's (S) cousin, took Rasulullah's (S) place in his bed. Rasūlullāh (S) went to his friend Abū Bakr's house, and together they headed towards Yathrib. He knew he would be safe in Yathrib.

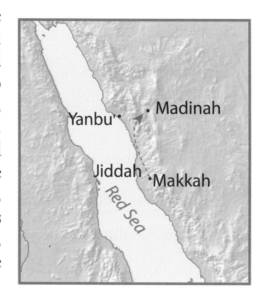

Points to Remember

- In 620 C.E., the first group of people came from Yathrib to Makkah.
- Six of the people in the first group accepted Islam.
- In 621 C.E., 12 people came from Yathrib and took the First Pledge of 'Aqabah.
- In 622 C.E., 75 people came from Yathrib, including two women.
- In 622 C.E., the Second Pledge of 'Aqabah was adopted.
- Al-'Abbās, the uncle of Rasūlullāh (S), was present during the signing of the pledge.

The Pledges of al-'Aqabah are very important in the history of Islam. Soon after the second pledge, in the year 622 C.E., Rasulullah (S) moved to Yathrib. If the people of Yathrib did not offer help to Muhammad (S), he could not have gone there for shelter. He had no other place to go. Without proper shelter, his life would have been in danger. The Pledges of al-'Aqabah provided a new opportunity for Islam. They created a new generation of Muslims who supported Prophet Muhammad (S) with their lives and wealth.

Note: C.E. stands for Common Era. The numbering of the year is identical to the A.D. system. Common Era is preferred because it does not have any religious titles referring to Jesus Christ.

1. How many people from Yathrib took the First Pledge of al-'Aqabah?

_____

2. How many people from Yathrib took the Second Pledge of al-'Aqabah?

_____

3. When were the First and the Second Pledges of al-'Aqabah taken?

   A. First Pledge in the year: _____

   B. Second Pledge in the year: _____

4. Circle T if the statement is true. Circle F if the statement is false.

   Uncle Abū Ṭālib was present at the time of the Pledge of al-'Aqabah.   T   F

   Uncle Al-'Abbās was present at the time of the Pledge of al-'Aqabah.   T   F

   The Pledge of al-'Aqabah was taken openly in front of the Ka'bah.   T   F

   The idol-worshippers also signed the Pledges of al-'Aqabah.   T   F

   Six men accepted Islam before any pledge of al-'Aqabah was taken.   T   F

5. How many years after the Second Pledge of al-'Aqabah did Rasūlullāh (S) secretly move out of Makkah?

   A.   Three years after the Second Pledge of al-'Aqabah.
   B.   Five years after the Second Pledge of al-'Aqabah.
   C.   The same year as the Second Pledge of al-'Aqabah.
   D.   One year before the Second Pledge of al-'Aqabah.

6. What was the main condition of the Second Pledge of al-'Aqabah?

   A.   The people of Yathrib would come for Hajj.
   B.   The people of Yathrib would love each other as Muslims.
   C.   The people of Yathrib would not give shelter to Muhammad (S).
   D.   The people of Yathrib would protect Muhammad (S) at any cost.

Hijrat to Madīnah: *The Migration that Shaped History*

Objective of the Lesson:

Rasūlullāh's (S) hijrat to Madīnah was very eventful. Students will learn what happened during the actual hijrat, when it took place, and who participated in the hijrat. This lesson provides an overview of the hijrat.

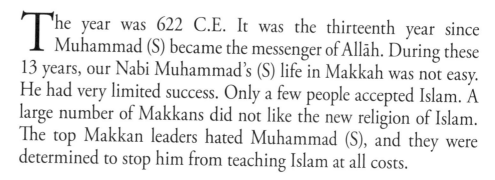

The year was 622 C.E. It was the thirteenth year since Muhammad (S) became the messenger of Allāh. During these 13 years, our Nabi Muhammad's (S) life in Makkah was not easy. He had very limited success. Only a few people accepted Islam. A large number of Makkans did not like the new religion of Islam. The top Makkan leaders hated Muhammad (S), and they were determined to stop him from teaching Islam at all costs.

In 622 C.E., Rasūlullāh (S) migrated from Makkah to Yathrib. This migration is known as **Hijrat**. The simple meaning of the word hijrat is to give up one's home and move to a different place to live.

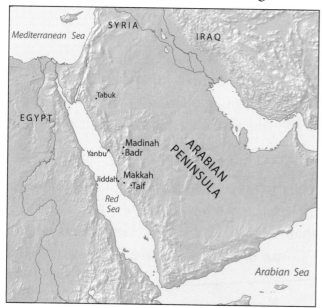

Prior development: In the previous lesson, we learned about the Pledges of al-ʿAqbah. These pledges gave new hope to our Nabi Muhammad (S) and other Muslims to find shelter in Yathrib.

A few years earlier, many Muslims migrated to Abyssinia when life in Makkah became difficult. In one sense, it was the first hijrat of the Muslims. Within a few years, most of them returned to Makkah. After the Pledges of Al-ʿAqabah, many Muslims had new hope and began migrating to Yathrib. Rasūlullāh (S) waited in Makkah to receive permission from Allāh to migrate.

Plan to kill Muhammad (S): The Makkan polytheists noticed that most Muslims were leaving Makkah. They realized Muhammad (S) might also leave. If he left Makkah, he might become powerful in a friendly community and create more problems for them. Therefore, the polytheists decided to kill him. They made a plan that one member from each of the nine clans of the Quraish tribe would stab him simultaneously and kill him. If everyone stabbed him at the same time, no single clan could be blamed.

Allāh had a greater plan: Rasūlullāh (S) received permission from Allāh to migrate. One night, the nine clan members assembled outside Rasūlullāh's (S) house to kill him. The people in Rasulullah's home realized the situation. To trick the killers, 'Ali slept on Rasūlullāh's (S) bed. Late in the night, Rasūlullāh (S) secretly left the house when the killers were sleepy. He went to his friend Abū Bakr's house, and together they began their hijrat to Madīnah.

A du'a of Rasulullah (S): As the hijrat would be difficult, Rasulullah (S) made a du'a to Allāh. He prayed:

$$\text{رَّبِّ أَدْخِلْنِي مُدْخَلَ صِدْقٍ وَأَخْرِجْنِي مُخْرَجَ صِدْقٍ}$$

$$\text{وَاجْعَل لِّي مِن لَّدُنكَ سُلْطَٰنًا نَّصِيرًا ۝}$$

Rabbi adkhilnī mudkhala sidqin wa akhrijnī mukhraja sidqin wa-j'al lī min ladunka sultanan nasīrā.

My Rabb! make me enter a truthful entering, and bring me out a truthful bringing out, and grant me from Yourself an authoritative help. (Bani Isra'il 17:80)

A wise move: Yathrib is about 200 miles north of Makkah. Rasūlullāh (S) and Abū Bakr knew if they moved northbound towards Yathrib, the killers would soon chase them and capture them. Therefore, to trick them, they moved south and hid inside a cave in a small mountain named **Thawr.**

Killers were fooled: Shortly before dawn, the nine clan members entered Rasūlullāh's (S) house to kill him. Before striking with their swords, one of the killers removed the blanket. They were shocked to find 'Ali on the bed. They realized Muhammad (S) had escaped. Immediately they sent search parties all over Makkah. They offered a prize of 100 camels to anyone who would capture Muhammad (S).

Incident near the cave: The search parties began looking all over the place. One man came close to the cave of Thawr. In the meantime, a spider had spun a web at the entrance of the cave. The entrance to the cave was bushy. A bird used the bushes to build her nest and laid an egg. The man looked at the spider web and thought that if anybody entered the cave, the web would have been torn. The web was not torn, so he thought the cave was empty. He also thought that if people were inside the cave, the bird would not have laid an egg on the nest right outside the cave. So he left. Had he looked inside, he could have seen the people inside.

> **Interesting Facts**
>
> The Thawr mountain is about 2,500 feet high.
>
> Spiders can have up to eight eyes, but they cannot see very well. They use vibration as the main sense.
>
> Spiders do not digest their food inside their stomach. The digestion is done outside the body!

Rasūlullāh (S) and Abū Bakr stayed inside the cave for three days. During this time, Abū Bakr's servant secretly brought them food at night. On the third night, a trustworthy guide brought two camels for them to ride. They mounted the camels and left for Yathrib in the darkness.

The journey: After a long and tiresome journey, Rasūlullāh (S) and Abū Bakr reached a place called **Qubā** near Yathrib. Rasūlullāh (S) began to build a mosque at Qubā. It was the first mosque ever built by the Muslims.

The people of Yathrib were anxiously waiting for Rasūlullāh (S) to arrive. After a few days, he entered Yathrib. The people were very happy and excited to see Rasūlullāh (S). In Yathrib, everybody wanted Rasūlullāh (S) to stay in their house. If he stayed in one person's house, another person might be offended. Therefore, he allowed his camel to choose where he would live. Wherever the camel would kneel down, that would be his residence. The camel knelt down on a piece of land owned by two orphans. Rasūlullāh (S) purchased the land from the orphans and built his home. Yathrib now became known as **Madinatun-Nabi**, or the City of the Nabi, or simply Madinah.

The hijrat of Rasūlullāh (S) started a new chapter in the history of Islam. Rasūlullāh (S) left Makkah after living there for 53 years. Now he began living in Madīnah as a ruler and an important person. The Islamic calendar begins with the first day of Hijrat. The year 622 C.E. is marked as the first year of Hijrah. Any year after Hijrah is indicated by the abbreviation A.H.

1. Before migration to Madīnah, some Muslims migrated to another country. What was the name of that country?

   _____

2. What is the simple meaning of the term hijrat as given in the lesson?

   _____

3. Fill in the blanks:

The year _____ C.E. is marked as the first year of the Islamic calendar. The Islamic calendar begins with the first day of Rasūlullāh's (S) _____ to Madīnah.

4. How long did Rasūlullāh (S) live in Makkah after receiving first revelation?

   A. Ten years.
   B. Thirteen years.
   C. Fifteen years.
   D. Twenty-five years.

5. In total, how long did Rasūlullāh (S) live in Makkah before migrating to Madīnah?

   A. Ten years.
   B. Twenty-five years.
   C. Forty years.
   D. Fifty-three years.

6. Circle T if the statement is true. Circle F if the statement is false.

Rasūlullāh (S) built a mosque in Qubā. It was the first mosque ever built by the Muslims.	T	F
The Makkans offered 200 camels to anyone who would capture Muhammad (S).	T	F
The cave of Thawr is located south of Makkah.	T	F
'Ali was lying on the bed of Muhammad (S) when the killers entered the house.	T	F

Madīnan Period: *Islam Prospers*

Objective of the Lesson:

This lesson provides a short summary of the Madīnan period. Many battles were fought during this period, and a large number of people accepted Islam. During these six short years, Islam evolved into a major religion, able to attract and influence the entire region.

The condition for Muslims in Makkah was unbearable. Many Muslims faced boycott in Makkah. Abū Lahab, the head of the tribe, opposed Muslims. Some Muslims migrated to Abyssinia. People of Tā'if did not accept the messages of Rasūlullāh (S). During this dark period, some people from Yathrib wanted Nabi Muhammad (S) to relocate to Yathrib and settle their disputes.

Pledges of al-'Aqaba and Hijrat: In the previous two lessons, we learned about the pledges of al-'Aqaba and the Hijrat. After Hijrat, Yathrib became Madinat-un-Nabi, or Madīnah. Madīnah was different from Makkah. It was much greener and the climate was better.

The Constitution: After the Muslims migrated to Madīnah, they were known as **muhājirūn** (مهاجر). The word means "those who migrated." The locals of Madīnah were known as **al-Ansārs** (الأنصار), or "the helpers." Several Arab and Jewish tribes lived in Madīnah. Sometimes they had peace, other times they fought. To establish peace, Rasūlullāh (S) issued a document known as the **Constitution of Madīnah**. The residents of Madīnah agreed to the rules in this document. This document described the duties and rights of the residents living in Madīnah.

Battle of Badr: As the power and authority of Nabi Muhammad (S) grew in Madīnah, the Quraish in Makkah became worried. For their business, they could not easily go to Syria through Madīnah. To destroy the Muslims and to improve the safety of their business travel, an army of Makkans attacked the Muslims. The leader was Abu Jahl. They had 1,000 soldiers, horses and camels, and they had better weapons than the Muslims. Some of the people in Madīnah became "hypocrites" (**munāfiq**). They helped the Quraish instead of helping their own people. Rasūlullāh (S) had only 313 poorly armed soldiers. He faced the enemies in a place called Badr. The Muslims won the battle. Abu Jahl died in the battle.

The victory of Badr greatly strengthened Rasūlullāh (S) and the Muslims. Rasūlullāh (S) was able to reach out to more tribes, and the number of Muslims increased. The hypocrites of Madīnah became weak.

Battle of Uhud: The following year, **Abū Sufyān**, a leader from Makkah, attacked the Muslims with 3,000 soldiers. A battle took place at Uhud. Initially, Muslims were winning the battle. Then some archers ignored the instructions of Rasūlullāh (S) and left an important battle position. As a result, the Muslims became a target of Makkan attack and they suffered a lot. Our beloved Rasūlullāh (S) was injured and fell unconscious. Muslims thought that Rasūlullāh (S) had passed away. They panicked and were about to give up the fight. Soon Rasūlullāh (S) regained consciousness, and the Muslims fought back. Nobody was a clear winner or loser.

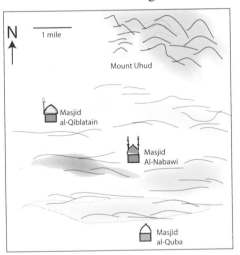

Battle of the Trench: Two years after the Battle of Uhud, Abū Sufyān led another army of 10,000 people. To protect the city, Rasulullah (S) had ordered a trench to be dug around Madīnah. The trench prevented the entry of the Quraish into Madīnah. For about a month, the Quraish waited outside Madīnah, as they could not cross the trench. They had not brought enough food for themselves or their animals to last a month. They were hungry and tired of waiting. Then, after a strong storm, the Makkan army gave up and left. Muslims won the Battle of the Trench without much bloodshed.

Treaty of Hudaibiyah: The next year, our Nabi Muhammad (S), with about 1,400 followers, proceeded to Makkah to perform the pilgrimage. The Makkans had planned to prevent the entry of the Muslims into the city. Rasulullah (S) camped at al-Hudaibiyah on the edge of Makkah. The Quraish learned that the Muslims wanted a peaceful pilgrimage. Yet they did not allow Rasulullah (S) to enter Makkah. An agreement, known as the **Treaty of Hudaibiyah,**

was signed. Muslims had to go back to Madīnah without performing the pilgrimage. They were very sad. Allāh (swt) told the Muslims that this treaty was actually a great victory.

$$ إِنَّا فَتَحْنَا لَكَ فَتْحًا مُّبِينًا ۝ $$

Surely We have given a victory to you—a Clear Victory. (Al-Fath 48:1)

Liberation of Makkah: Within a year of signing the Treaty of Hudaibiyah, the Makkans broke the treaty. In 630 C.E., Rasūlullāh Muhammad (S) marched to Makkah with 10,000 followers. The Quraish leaders could not resist and could not fight. Rasūlullāh (S) forgave them for all the bad things that they had done to the Muslims. The Makkans were touched by this kindness, and almost all of them became Muslim. The idols in the Ka'bah were destroyed. The Ka'bah then became free of *shirk* (setting partners with Allāh).

After Makkah was liberated, most of the tribes of Arabia started becoming Muslim. Before hijrah, our Rasūl Muhammad (S) did not have many followers. Ten years later, almost half of Arabia was under his control. What a blessing from Allāh (swt)!

The final days of the Greatest Man: In 632 C.E., Rasūlullāh Muhammad (S) led a pilgrimage of Hajj to Makkah. After Hajj, he went back to Madīnah. He was in poor health for some time. In June 632 C.E., our beloved Rasulullah (S) passed away. He was 63 years old. He had fulfilled his duty of preaching the Truth.

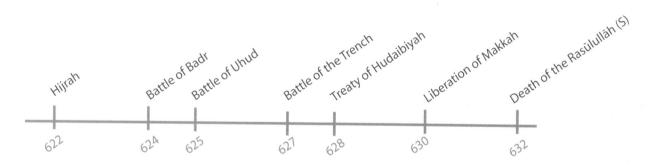

Timeline of Rasūlullāh's (S) life in Madīnah

1. The migration to Madīnah became possible when the people of Yathrib made two pledges. What are the names of the two pledges?

1. _____ 2. _____

2. What were the Makkan Muslims, who arrived in Madīnah, called?

_____

3. What were the Madinan people, who gave shelter to the Muslims from Makkah, called?

_____

4. Name the three battles that the Muslims fought against the Makkans. Write them in the order they were fought.

1) _____

2) _____

3) _____

5. Which battle did the Muslims fight with only a 313-man army?

_____

6. What was the name of the treaty that later helped the liberation of Makkah?

_____

Liberation of Makkah

Objective of the Lesson:

Within six years from the date of migration to Madīnah, Muslims were able to liberate Makkah. How did it happen? This lesson provides a short summary of what led to the victory march and how Muslims were able to conquer the land of enemies without shedding any blood.

In the previous lessons, we learned that in 622 C.E., Rasūlullāh (S) secretly moved to Madīnah to avoid the Makkan polytheists. We also learned that in 628 C.E., he decided to travel to Makkah to perform Hajj. The polytheists prevented him from entering Makkah, and they made a contract known as the Treaty of Hudaibiyah. The Makkans told the Muslims to go back to Madīnah without performing Hajj, but they could come back next year only for the purpose of umrah. Umrah is a shorter and simpler form of Hajj. They also agreed to keep peace for ten years. During these ten years, nobody would kill another. Although Rasūlullāh (S) wanted to perform Hajj, he went back to Madīnah after signing the Treaty of Hudaibiyah.

Most Muslims were unhappy because they could not perform Hajj. They thought the treaty was a defeat for them. Allāh told them it was a Great Victory for them, even though they did not understand how it was a success.

Makkans break the treaty: In little over a year after signing the treaty, a Makkan tribe killed two men of a tribe that were allies to Muslims. According to the treaty, they were not supposed to kill each other. Now that the

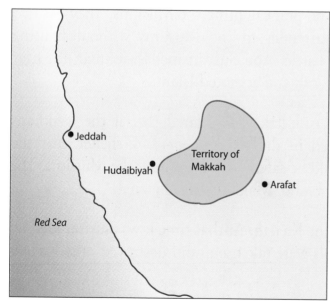

Jeddah

Hudaibiyah

Territory of Makkah

Arafat

Red Sea

Makkans had killed two men allied to the Muslims, Rasūlullāh (S) declared the treaty cancelled.

Abū Sufyān comes to Madīnah: When the Makkan leaders realized the treaty was cancelled, they became nervous. Abū Sufyān, the leader of the Quraish, came to Madīnah to say that they were sorry for killing the Muslims and promised to follow the treaty. Rasūlullāh (S) did not listen to Abū Sufyān. There was no guarantee that they would not break the treaty again. Abū Sufyān tried everything to make the Muslims believe he would follow the treaty, but the Muslims refused to listen to him or trust him. Abū Sufyān returned to Makkah. He was very worried.

Rasūlullāh (S) arrives in Makkah: In the month of Ramadan in 630 C.E., Rasūlullāh (S) began his journey to liberate Makkah from idol-worshipping. He was accompanied by 10,000

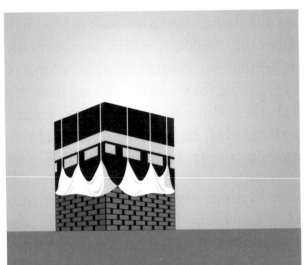

companions. The journey was kept top secret. Only when the Muslims were very close to Makkah, did the Makkans learn about their arrival. They did not expect this to happen. They were totally surprised. The Makkans felt helpless in front of the large Muslim gathering. They realized there was no point fighting the Muslims. They decided to surrender to the Muslims without fighting any battle. Abū Sufyān met Rasūlullāh (S) near Makkah and accepted Islam.

Rasūlullāh (S) declared that if the Makkans stayed in their houses, or took shelter near the Ka'bah or in the house of Abū Sufyān, they would be safe. Nobody resisted the Muslims. The Muslims entered Makkah without shedding any blood. Makkah was liberated.

The Ka'bah was purified: Rasūlullāh (S) went to the Ka'bah. At that time it was surrounded by a large number of idols. One by one, all the idols were taken out and destroyed. The Ka'bah and the area around it were purified.

Extraordinary mercy: The Makkans thought that Nabi Muhammad (S) might punish them for the years of enmity towards the Muslims. After the liberation of Makkah, Rasūlullāh (S) pardoned the entire community of Makkah. The Quraish in Makkah could not believe it. They were thrilled! Many of them cried in joy. All these years they hated Muhammad (S), they drove him out of Makkah, and they even tried to kill him. However, when our Nabi Muhammad (S) had the chance, he did not seek revenge. The generosity of our Nabi Muhammad (S) won the hearts of the idol-worshippers. They came forward and accepted Islam.

Makkah became a place free of hatred and enmity. It became a city of Muslims.

Points to Ponder
The power of forgiveness is greater than the power of revenge. How did this act of forgiveness by Rasūlullāh (S) ultimately benefit Islam?
Rasūlullāh (S) was determined and strict, yet he was very kind and loving. During the liberation of Makkah, what were the ways he showed his determination, strictness, kindness, and love?

1. In which year did Rasūlullāh (S) liberate Makkah?

    A.   622 C.E.
    B.   625 C.E.
    C.   630 C.E.
    D.   632 C.E.

2. Circle T if the sentence is true. Circle F if the sentence is false.

The Treaty of Hudaibiyah was signed in 628 C.E.	T	F
The Treaty of Hudaibiyah required all to maintain peace for ten years.	T	F
The Makkans broke the Treaty of Hudaibiyah.	T	F
When the Muslims liberated Makkah, they killed a large number of people.	T	F
Rasūlullāh (S) let some idols remain around the Ka'bah.	T	F

3. When Abū Sufyān realized the Treaty of Hudaibiyah was cancelled, what did he do?

_____

4. After Makkah was liberated, how did Rasūlullāh (S) treat his Quraish enemies?

_____

5. How many Muslims marched to liberate Makkah?

    A.   1,000 Muslims.
    B.   5,000 Muslims.
    C.   10,000 Muslims.
    D.   100,000 Muslims.

Abū Bakr (R): *The First Khalīfah*

Objective of the Lesson:

After Rasūlullāh (S) passed away, Abū Bakr became the first Khalīfah. In this lesson, students will learn about Abū Bakr as a friend, guide, and constant companion of Rasūlullāh (S).

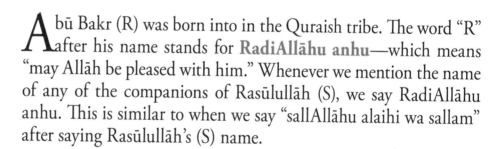

Abū Bakr (R) was born into in the Quraish tribe. The word "R" after his name stands for **RadiAllāhu anhu**—which means "may Allāh be pleased with him." Whenever we mention the name of any of the companions of Rasūlullāh (S), we say RadiAllāhu anhu. This is similar to when we say "sallAllāhu alaihi wa sallam" after saying Rasūlullāh's (S) name.

Abū Bakr (R) was a few years younger than our Nabi Muhammad (S). After Rasūlullāh (S) received revelation from Allāh, the first person to become a Muslim was his wife Khadījah (ra). After Khadījah (ra) the next adult to accept Islam was Abū Bakr (R). Thus, he was the first man to accept Islam. He was a lifelong partner and a good friend of our Prophet (S).

Honest and generous: Abū Bakr was a rich person. He used his wealth to help those who became Muslim. He spent his money to free many slaves. Once Rasūlullāh (S) needed money to fight the Romans. Abū Bakr donated all his wealth. Rasūlullāh (S) asked him if he kept anything for himself. He replied that he kept only Allāh and the messenger of Allāh. He was fondly named **as-Siddiq**, or "the honest one."

Hijrat: When Rasūlullāh (S) decided to migrate to Madīnah, Abū Bakr accompanied him. Together they hid inside a cave named **Thawr** while the Makkans searched for them. They stayed in the cave for three days and then secretly moved to Madīnah. He was the first person to migrate to Madīnah along with Rasūlullāh (S).

Close companion: During all the important battles, Abū Bakr fought in the Muslim army. People respected him. Rasūlullāh (S) liked him for his kindness and good-natured heart. When Rasūlullāh (S) was very sick and could not lead the prayers, he asked Abū Bakr to lead the prayer. Such was his respect and position among the Muslims.

Abū Bakr had two daughters, Asma and 'A'ishah. Rasūlullāh (S) married 'A'ishah (ra). Thus, Abū Bakr became his father-in-law.

Appointment as a Khalīfah: As long as Rasūlullāh (S) was alive, he was the leader of the Muslims. All the Muslims followed his command. But after Rasūlullāh (S) passed away, the Muslims needed a new leader. They thought that if a leader was not chosen quickly, the community would have problems. The companions discussed among themselves and decided to appoint Abū Bakr as the leader of the Muslims.

The leader is called **Khalīfah**. Abū Bakr became the first khalīfah of the Muslims. There were four such khalīfahs. These khalīfahs were appointed by the Muslims and they were guided by the teachings of Allāh and the Messenger. Therefore, they were called **Khulafa-e Rashidun**. This means "Rightly Guided Khalīfahs."

Abū Bakr's rule: As a Rightly Guided Khalīfah, Abū Bakr ruled for only two years before he passed away. During these two years, Abū Bakr completed many important tasks. The most important task was to save the Muslim community from breaking apart. Soon after Rasūlullāh's (S) death, many Muslims thought there was no need to follow Islam. Many of them gave up the religion. Many of them plotted against Islam. Abū Bakr brought them back to Islam and punished those who plotted against Islam.

Soon after the death of Rasūlullāh (S), a few people claimed that they were new prophets of Allāh. But there cannot be any new prophets of Allāh.[33:40] These were false claims. However, they were able to attract quite a few followers. Abū Bakr sent armies against these people and punished them for saying such things.

Soon after the death of Rasūlullāh (S), many tribes in faraway places declared themselves free nations. Abū Bakr sent armies against these tribes to bring them back to Islam or fight them for their wrongdoing. Soon he made all of Arabia a strong Muslim country. The boundaries of Islam continued to expand during his rule.

Another important thing that Abū Bakr did was to compile the entire Qur'ān into a single book. Until that time, the Qur'ān was not formally compiled into a book. He compiled the Qur'ān and placed the copy under the care of one of the wives of Rasūlullāh (S).

End of an era: Abū Bakr passed away in 634 C.E. Before his death, he was able to strengthen the position of Muslims. His personality, leadership qualities, and vision kept Muslims united. Abū Bakr will be forever remembered in the history of Islam as a great companion.

Points to Ponder

None of the four khalifas names are mentioned in the Qur'ān. If the Qur'ān was written by Nabi Muhammad (S), would he not have included the names of his near and dear companions? The fact that the names of these companions are not in the Qur'ān indicates that it was not written by Muhammad (S).

If Abū Bakr had not consolidated the position of Islam after the death of Rasūlullāh (S), what would have possibly happened to Islam?

1. Who was the first Khulafa-e Rashidun?

   _____

2. Write the name of Abū Bakr's daughter who married Prophet Muhammad (S).

   _____

3. Who appointed Abū Bakr as leader of the Muslims?

   _____

4. When Rasūlullāh (S) migrated to Madīnah, in which cave did he hide with Abū Bakr?

   _____

5. Circle T if the sentence is true. Circle F if the sentence is false.

   Abū Bakr had lots of wealth, which he used to help the Muslims.   T   F

   Abū Bakr ordered the compilation of the Qur'ān.   T   F

   Abū Bakr ruled for five years as the leader of the Muslims.   T   F

4. Find the following words in the word search below: ROMANS, ABU BAKR, KHALIFA, THAWR, ISLAM, AISHAH, MADINAH, KABAH, RELIGION, MAKKAH, LEADER.

A	L	R	O	M	A	N	S	R	A
M	E	N	D	R	B	A	B	E	I
A	A	A	G	M	U	G	O	L	S
D	D	I	K	A	B	A	H	I	L
I	E	S	T	H	A	W	R	G	A
N	R	H	A	H	K	N	K	I	M
A	R	A	B	Q	R	J	L	O	W
H	K	H	A	L	I	F	A	N	A
B	N	W	M	A	K	K	A	H	C

'Umar al-Khattāb (R): *The Second Khalīfah*

Objective of the Lesson:

In this lesson students will learn about 'Umar al Khattab, the second Khalīfah. Students will learn about how 'Umar accepted Islam. This lesson also provides a short summary of his entire life and major achievements.

Sixteen years after the birth of our Messenger Muhammad (S), 'Umar Ibn al-Khattāb (R) was born into the famous Quraish tribe. His father's name was **al-Khattāb**. Much later, after 'Umar Ibn al-Khattāb accepted Islam, he became known as **al-Fārūq** and **Amir al-Mu'minin** due to his outstanding qualities.

'Umar was an outspoken, fearless, and determined person. People feared him because of his commanding personality. When Rasūlullāh (S) received the first revelation in 610 C.E., 'Umar was a 24-year-old man. He did not believe in the teachings of Muhammad (S) and he did not like Islam or Muslims. He was a polytheist, which means he worshipped idols. He considered Muhammad (S) an enemy of Makkah for teaching Islam.

'Umar accepts Islam: An incident happened about six years after Muhammad (S) became Rasūlullāh. One day, 'Umar became very angry when people were talking about Islam. He decided to kill Muhammad (S) and stop his teachings. He left with a sword, but someone told him he should first check his own household because his own sister had become a Muslim. On hearing this, 'Umar became more angry and decided to kill his sister first. At his sister's house, he heard the recitation of a sūrah. He demanded to know what they were reading. His sister and her husband refused to answer. Then 'Umar struck his sister and her husband. She fell down injured and started bleeding. On seeing the blood, 'Umar became sad. But he still demanded to know what they were reading. Then they told him it was a sūrah from the Qur'ān. He wanted to read it, but his sister told him he should clean himself before touching it. After he cleansed himself and began reading the sūrah, he became fascinated with what he was reading. He could not stop reading the wonderful verses. He immediately decided to accept Islam. He went to Rasūlullāh (S) and declared his faith in Islam. Moments earlier he wanted to kill Muhammad (S), and now he wanted to become a believer. If Allāh wishes, and if we show interest, Allāh can make wonderful things happen in our lives.

'Umar's acceptance of Islam gave the new Muslims lots of support and courage. Since that time, 'Umar became one of the main advisers to Rasūlullāh (S) in all important matters.

Family ties with Rasūlullāh (S): 'Umar had a daughter named Hafsa (ra). When she became a widow, Rasūlullāh (S) married her. Until this time 'Umar was only a friend and companion of Rasūlullāh (S). Now he became his father-in-law. Hafsa (ra) was a very pious and wise woman.

The second Khalīfah: After Muhammad (S) died in 632 C.E., Abū Bakr became the Khalīfah of the Muslim world. But within two years, Abū Bakr passed away. Before his death, he appointed 'Umar as Khalīfah of the Muslim world. As a Khalīfah, 'Umar ruled for ten years.

'Umar continued the good work of Abū Bakr. He was a very strict and able administrator. He continued to expand the Muslim Empire. He had defeated the two major powers at that time—the Persians and the Romans.

'Umar's achievements: The list of 'Umar's major achievements is endless. He started the Islamic calendar from the date of migration of Rasūlullāh (S). He began the survey and assessment of lands for collecting taxes. He established the Land Revenue Department. He established military bases at strategic points in different provinces. He made sure the poor among the Jews and Christians who lived in conquered lands received regular money from the government. He began *tarawih* (Ramadan night prayers) in congregations. Previously, before his time, these prayers were made individually. The list goes on and on.

In 644 C.E., 'Umar was killed by a Persian slave named Fīroz.

1. When 'Umar (r) heard that his sister became a Muslim, he went to her house. Why did he go to his sister's house?

_____

2. At his sister's house, 'Umar (r) began reading a sūrah. What happened to him after he read the sūrah?

_____

3. Who was the Khalīfah of the Muslim world immediately before 'Umar (r) became the Khalīfah?

_____

4. Circle T if the sentence is correct. Circle F if the sentence is false.

In his early life, 'Umar (r) was a polytheist.	T	F
'Umar's daughter was 'A'ishah (ra).	T	F
'Umar (r) defeated the mighty Romans.	T	F
'Umar (r) defeated the mighty Persians.	T	F

5. Name 'Umar's (r) three major achievements as the Khalīfah.

1. _____

2. _____

3. _____

6. Find the following words in the word search puzzle below: UMAR, KHALIFA, HAFSA, SURAH, ISLAM, MUHAMMAD, AL KHATTAB, EMPIRE, POLYTHEIST, KILL, FIROZ

D	A	L	K	H	A	T	T	A	B
A	F	H	I	O	S	U	R	A	H
H	Q	H	L	T	W	M	Q	E	A
K	H	A	L	I	F	A	A	M	F
R	T	F	A	S	H	R	S	P	I
I	A	S	T	L	K	A	P	I	R
W	O	A	U	A	N	M	L	R	O
M	U	H	A	M	M	A	D	E	Z
P	O	L	Y	T	H	E	I	S	T

'Uthmān ibn 'Affān (R): *The Third Khalīfah*

Objective of the Lesson:

'Uthmān was the third Khalīfah of the Islamic state. As a Khalīfah, his contribution to the promotion of Islam was very important. Several key events happened during his rule. This lesson provides a short summary of the life and achievements of this Khalīfah.

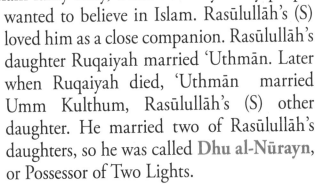

Uthmān ibn 'Affān (R) was born into the powerful Umayyad clan of Makkah. He was six years younger than Rasūlullāh (S). At a very young age, he began trading merchandise in different places. This business brought him a lot of wealth. He was a very kind-hearted and generous person.

Uthman accepted Islam upon the invitation of his friend Abū Bakr. He accepted Islam fairly early, when not very many people wanted to believe in Islam. Rasūlullāh's (S) loved him as a close companion. Rasūlullāh's daughter Ruqaiyah married 'Uthmān. Later when Ruqaiyah died, 'Uthmān married Umm Kulthum, Rasūlullāh's (S) other daughter. He married two of Rasūlullāh's daughters, so he was called **Dhu al-Nūrayn**, or Possessor of Two Lights.

During his early life, he migrated twice. The first migration was to Abyssinia, when Rasūlullāh (S) sent several Muslims there to seek protection. His second migration was to Madīnah, when all Muslims gave up their homes in Makkah and settled in Madīnah.

At the time of the Hudaibiyah negotiations, the Makkans prevented the Muslims from performing Hajj. At that time, Rasūlullāh (S) sent 'Uthmān to the Quraish camp to negotiate for the Muslims. The Quraish allowed 'Uthmān to perform Umrah, but they would not allow the Muslims to do so. 'Uthmān refused to do it unless all Muslims were allowed. The Quraish held him as a hostage for several days in Makkah. The Muslims did not know his whereabouts and feared that he had been killed. Finally he returned and the Muslims were relieved.

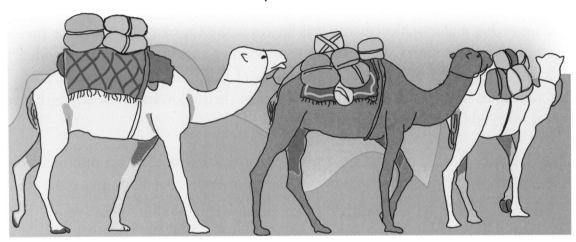

'Uthmān's generosity: Islamic history describes a famous account of the generosity of 'Uthmān. Once he received a large caravan from Damascus carrying food and other goods. All the local merchants gathered at his house and asked him to sell them some of the items he received. 'Uthmān told them he would sell only if he received a good price. Each merchant offered him a high price, but 'Uthmān kept on asking for a higher price. Finally they offered him the highest price they could pay and told him that no merchant would be able to pay him more than what they had offered. Then 'Uthmān told them he would sell the goods to the one who would give him ten times what the other merchants were offering. He meant that he would sell the goods to Allāh because Allāh promises to multiply any charity 700 times.[2:261] Then 'Uthmān gave the entire caravan to the starving people of Madīnah and did not charge them anything. There are many other accounts of his generosity.

'Uthmān becomes Khalīfah: After 'Umar, the second Khalīfah, was assassinated, the companions selected 'Uthmān to become the third Khalīfah of the Islamic state. As Khalīfah, he ruled for ten years. During 'Umar's rule, the Islamic state expanded beyond the borders of the Arab Peninsula

Interesting Facts

'Uthmān belonged to the Umayyad clan.

'Uthmān married Rasūlullāh's (S) daughter Ruqaiyah.

Later when Ruqaiyah died, 'Uthmān married Umm Kulthum, Rasūlullāh's (S) another daughter.

'Uthmān circulated official copies of the Qur'ān.

'Uthmān was killed by an angry group of people.

'Uthmān ruled for ten years.

into Egypt, Syria, and Iraq. During 'Uthmān's rule, the Islamic state expanded into Persia, parts of India, parts of Russia, Turkey, and across North Africa and the corners of China. Under his rule, the Islamic state became rich and powerful. Many people from the new regions accepted Islam.

Life as a Khalīfah: 'Uthmān was a rich person. but he led a simple life. Even after becoming Khalīfah of the Islamic state, he led a simple life. He never took salary for his service as Khalīfah. One of his major achievements was to copy the Qur'ān and circulate the copies to different parts of the country. He took care of widows and orphans and provided them generous charity. During his rule, some of the wives of Rasūlullāh (S) were still alive. They received an allowance from the State. 'Uthmān doubled their allowance. He strengthened the Muslim naval force and defeated the Romans.

Final years of trouble: During the last six years of his rule, 'Uthmān faced internal problems and troubles. Many Muslims complained that 'Uthmān appointed famous people from his own Umayyad clan to top government positions. People often complained that he was too kind to be a good ruler. During his rule, many people became his enemies, but he never took strong action against them. He was a merciful ruler. When he realized his life was in danger, he did not use state money to protect himself or his family. The enemies continued to make his administration difficult by opposing everything he wanted to do. They continued to accuse him of showing favor to his own clan. Ultimately, due to this reason, 'Uthmān was assassinated by an angry mob. It is reported that he was killed while reading the Qur'ān. After his assassination, widespread disagreement, called *fitnah*, broke out among the Muslims.

1. As Khalīfah of the Islamic world, how long did ʿUthmān rule?

    A.   Two years.
    B.   Ten years.
    C.   Fifteen years.
    D.   Thirty-two years.

2. What was one of ʿUthmān's major achievements during his life?

    _____

3. ʿUthmān married two of Rasūlullāh's (S) daughters. Name the two daughters.

    1)   _____

    2)   _____

4. What were the two complaints people made about ʿUthmān's rule?

    1)   _____

    2)   _____

5. Name some of the territories that were occupied during ʿUthmān's rule.

    _____

    _____

6. Circle T if the sentence is true. Circle F if the sentence is false.

    A. ʿUthmān was younger than Nabi Muhammad (S).   T   F

    B. At one time, ʿUthmān was held as a hostage by the Quraish.   T   F

    C. ʿUthmān was the first Khalīfah to be assassinated.   T   F

    D. ʿUthmān belonged to the Abbasid clan.   T   F

'Ali Ibn Abu Tālib (R): *The Fourth Khalīfah*

Objective of the Lesson:

'Ali was the last of the four rightly guided Khalīfah in Islam. During his rule, people had many conflicts. Some Muslim groups opposed other Muslim groups. This lesson provides a short overview of the life and achievements of this Khalīfah.

In the year 600 C.E., 'Ali (R) was born in Makkah to a noble Quraish family. His father, Abū Tālib, was a Quraish leader and had many responsibilities. Although he was the leader, he was not very wealthy. With his meager income, he had difficulty in maintaining his family.

When 'Ali was born, Muhammad (S) was 30 years old and already married to Khadījah (ra). She was a wealthy person. Seeing the financial difficulties of his uncle Abū Tālib, Muhammad (S) offered to look after 'Ali. It was thought that 'Ali would receive good care and comfort in Muhammad's (S) household.

When Muhammad (S) was a child, his uncle, Abū Tālib, became his guardian and protector. Even when Muhammad (S) was 30 years old, Abū Tālib continued to be his guardian and protector. By taking care of 'Ali, Muhammad (S) found an opportunity to express thanks to his uncle.

First youth to accept Islam: In 610 C.E. when Muhammad (S) received the call from Allāh to become a Rasūl, 'Ali was about 10 years old. He did not understand a lot about what it meant to be a messenger of Allāh, but he trusted his cousin Muhammad (S) and accepted Islam. He was the first young boy to accept Islam. He continued to live in Rasūlullāh's (S) household until he was a young man. He had the rare opportunity to watch Muhammad (S) both as a Rasūl and as a family man.

Just before the Hijrah, when the nonbelievers came to kill Rasūlullāh (S), 'Ali slept in Rasūlullāh's (S) the bed. Rasūlullāh (S) assured 'Ali that no harm would come to him. 'Ali knew it was dangerous, but he also knew he could not be killed. 'Ali did not hesitate and took the risk of his life. Such was his love for Nabi Muhammad (S) and the cause of Islam.

Marriage of 'Ali: After 'Ali migrated to Madīnah, he married Rasūlullāh's daughter Fātimah. 'Ali was Rasūlullāh's (S) first cousin. After 'Ali married Rasūlullāh's (S) daughter, he became his son-in-law. Rasūlullāh (S) had special love for his daughter Fātimah, thus his love for 'Ali was also great.

'Ali and Fātimah lived a very simple life. Often they did not have food to eat, but they did not complain. They had three sons and two daughters. One of their sons died during infancy. Two other sons were Al-Hasan and Al-Husain. Rasūlullāh (S) loved them very much and often played with them. When they grew up, they became Imams, or religious leaders.

Two titles for 'Ali: 'Ali was a good warrior. He fought in many battles. Nobody could defeat him in sword fighting. Due to his courage in battles, Rasūlullāh (S) named him **Asadullah**, or Lion of Allāh.

'Ali loved education and knowledge. When the Qur'ān was revealed, he wrote down the revelations many times for Rasūlullāh (S), who did not know how to write. 'Ali was fondly given the title **Bābul 'Ilm**, which means "The Door of Knowledge."

Ali becomes a Khalīfah: 'Ali was a good leader. In 656 C.E., he became the fourth Khalīfah after a mob killed 'Uthmān. 'Ali was 56 years old at that time. As a Khalīfah, he ruled for almost five years. He was the last of the four Rightly Guided Khalīfahs in Islam. After his death, many other Khalīfahs ruled the Muslims, but none of them were called Rightly Guided.

When 'Ali became the Khalīfah, the Muslims were divided into two groups. One group liked 'Ali and the other group wanted to fight him. Two of the main reasons for their disagreement were whether 'Ali was the right candidate for the Khalīfah. The other reason was whether 'Ali was doing enough to punish those who killed 'Uthmān, the third Khalīfah. 'Ali tried to make both groups happy and tried to solve their problems. During his short rule as Khalīfah, 'Ali had to fight a few battles—all for political reasons.

One such battle was known as the **Battle of the Camel**. In this battle, Rasūlullāh's (S) widow, 'A'ishah, fought 'Ali. The main purpose of the battle was to find and punish the culprits who killed 'Uthmān. 'A'ishah thought that 'Ali was not doing enough to capture and punish the murderers. After this battle, 'Ali moved his capital from Madinah to Kūfa. Kūfa is a city in present-day Iraq.

In another battle, known as the **Battle of Siffin**, fought one year after the Battle of the Camel, 'Ali fought Mu'āwiyah. The main reason for this battle, started by Mu'āwiyah, was also to seek revenge for the murder of 'Uthmān. Mu'āwiyah also thought that 'Ali was not doing enough to punish the culprits. These battles caused much bloodshed and a large number of Muslims were killed.

One day when 'Ali was praying in a mosque in the city of Kūfa, a man stabbed him. 'Ali died from his injury. He was 61 years old.

1. How old was 'Ali (R) when Muhammad (S) became a Rasūl?

    A.   Five years old.
    B.   Ten years old.
    C.   Fifteen years old.
    D.   Thirty years old.

2. Name the two sons of 'Ali (R) with whom Rasūlullāh (S) used to play.

    _____

3. Circle T if the sentence is true. Circle F if the sentence is false.

Like Rasūlullāh (S), 'Ali also could not read and write.	T	F
Abū Tālib was a cousin of 'Ali.	T	F
'Ali ruled as a Khalīfah for almost five years.	T	F
Like Abū Bakr and 'Uthmān, 'Ali was also a wealthy person.	T	F

4. Write the two titles that were given to 'Ali.

    1)   _____

    2)   _____

5. Find the following words in the word search puzzle below:

KHALIFA, ABU TALIB, FATIMAH, GUARDIAN, CAMEL, BATTLE,
BLANKET, MAKKAH, IMAM, KUFA,

A	G	E	Q	R	K	U	F	A	M
E	U	K	H	A	L	I	F	A	A
C	A	M	E	L	E	Y	A	B	K
R	R	D	K	T	D	U	H	U	K
O	D	H	T	Y	C	J	N	T	A
G	I	J	F	A	T	I	M	A	H
B	A	T	T	L	E	S	A	L	O
A	N	K	W	I	M	A	M	I	Y
H	B	L	A	N	K	E	T	B	P

Compilers of Hadīth

Objective of the Lesson:

This lesson provides a short overview of the main compilers of Hadīth. These compilers devoted their entire lives to carefully and methodically collecting the sayings of Rasūlullāh (S).

When Messenger Muhammad (S) was alive, many people watched him to hear what he said and see what he did. People tried to remember the words and actions of Rasūlullāh (S), and they told others who were not around Rasūlullāh (S). The description of the words of Rasūlullāh (S) is known as Hadīth. If we are talking about more than one hadīth, we call them **ahādīth**. The actions of Rasūlullāh (S) are known as the **Sunnah**.

As time passed, many people from different parts of the world became Muslim. Many of these people had never seen Rasūlullāh (S). They were always eager to know how Muhammad (S) lived and his actions. They learned about the life of Rasūlullāh (S) through people who had seen him. As time passed, the people who had seen Rasūlullāh (S) also passed away. Now people thought that they would slowly forget what Rasūlullāh (S) did and said. They felt that they should write down what people remembered.

The following chart shows the year of birth and death of the six most honored compilers of ahādīth. The six collections of ahādīth are known as *As-Sahih sitta*, the "true six."

Compiler	Dates of life	Compilation
Imam Muhammad ibn Ismail al-Bukhārī	194–256 A.H.	Sahih Bukhārī
Imam Muslim ibn al-Hajjaj	204–261 A.H.	Sahih Muslim
Allamah Abu Dawūd Sulaiman	202–275 A.H.	Sunan Abi Dawūd
Allamah Abu 'Isa Tirmidhī	209–289 A.H.	Sunan al-Tirmidhī
Allamah Ahmad an-Nasā'ī	210–303 A.H.	Sunan al-Sughra
Allamah Ibn Mājāh	209–273 A.H.	Sunan Ibn Mājāh

Imam Bukhārī: He was born in Bukhara in present-day Uzbekistan. He was born about 170 years after Rasūlullāh (S). During his childhood he was blind, but he later regained his vision. He had a remarkable memory and could narrate thousands of ahādīth accurately. During his lifetime, he memorized more than 300,000 ahādīth. From this collection, he discarded most, as he was not sure about the narrators. He kept about 7,000 ahādīth. These are known as Sahih, or true hadīth.

Bukhārī was highly respected for his extraordinary intellect. He traveled to Nishapur, Samarkand, and Baghdad. Wherever he went, people liked him. However, in each place, some people became jealous of him and banished him.

Imam Muslim: Imam Muslim was born in Nishapur, Persia. He traveled extensively in Arabia, Egypt, Syria, and Iraq collecting ahādīth. He had many students who helped him collect ahādīth. In his collection, many hadīth are Sahih ahādīth. He collected ahādīth after Imam al-Bukhari.

Abu Dawūd: He was a famous collector of ahādīth. He was born in Sijistan, Iran. Like all other hadīth collectors, he also traveled widely. He was mainly interested in law, and as a result, his collection mainly focuses on legal ahādīth. He collected about 50,000 ahādīth from which he chose 4,800 for compilation.

Tirmidhī: He was a student of Imam Muslim and Abu Dawūd. Not many details can be found about his life. He lived in Khorasan, Iraq, and Hejaz. Most of the ahādīth he collected are related to law, rules, and regulations.

Nasā'ī: He was a famous collector of ahādīth. He was born in Nasā (in Khorasan) and traveled extensively to collect ahādīth. He lived in Egypt for a while and then in Damascus. He died in 915 C.E. His collection is known as Sunan al-Sughra or Sunan an-Nasā'ī.

Ibn Mājāh: He collected about 4,000 ahādīth and compiled them into 32 volumes. Today his work is not as equally valued as the works of Bukhārī or Muslim. Some of his collections appear to be weak because scholars cannot agree on the authenticity of the collection.

Each hadīth has two parts. The transmission of hadīth through a chain of many narrators is the **isnad**. The content of the hadīth is the text, or **matn**. Depending on the reliability of the isnad, some hadīth are considered reliable, some are weak, and others are poor or unreliable.

Not all the recorded ahādīth or sunnah describe only the sayings or actions of Rasūlullāh (S). Some of the recordings also describe the sayings or ways of life of Rasūlullāh's (S) companions.

All of the words in the Qur'ān are directly from Allāh (swt). A hadīth is not the word of Allāh. Therefore, Qur'ān is the main book of the Islamic religion. The position of the hadīth collections is below the Qur'ān.

1. What was the main mode of transmitting hadīth at the time of Rasūlullāh (S)?

_____

2. What does the term *Sahih Sittah* mean?

_____

3. Write down the names of the six major Imams whose work is known as the *Sahih Sittah*.

1) _____

2) _____

3) _____

4) _____

5) _____

6) _____

4. In a hadīth, what are *isnad* and *matn*. Explain your answer.

_____

_____

Shaitān's Mode of Operation

Objective of the Lesson:

Allāh created Shaitān to test us. Allāh wants us to stay away from Shaitān because he is our open enemy. Students will learn about the way Shaitān works. They will learn how to identify Shaitān's temptations and how to avoid his call.

Allāh (swt) tells us in the Qur'ān that our biggest enemy is Shaitān.[12:5; 17:53; 35:6]

And say to My servants that they speak that which is the best. Surely Shaitān stirs up quarrels among them. Shaitān is certainly a clear enemy towards mankind. (17:53)

Allāh wants us to stay away from the temptations of Shaitān. We have to be careful as Shaitān is invisible. He can see us, but we cannot see him. The big question is: how can we tell Shaitān is trying to tempt us? The only way we can know him is if we know how he operates. Once we know him through his actions, it will be possible for us to stay away from him.

What Shaitān does not look like: When we talk about Shaitān, we usually tend to think of an evil monster or devil who wants to scare us. We tend to think he is like a ghost, always waiting in the dark to play pranks on us. We may picture him with two horns on his head, big teeth, and a scary look. These are the imaginations of people. We really do not know what he looks like. Therefore, scary looks or horns on his head are pure imagination.

One thing is true about Shaitān—he pretends to be very friendly with us. If he had scary looks, we probably would not be friends with him. If he waited in the dark to scare us, we would be afraid of him. Therefore, he does not have a scary look.

Shaitān whispers in our minds: Shaitān wants to mislead us from the right path—the path shown by Allāh. If Shaitān simply told us to go down the wrong path, we would not listen. Therefore, to make us listen to him, he pretends to be our good friend. He pretends that he wants the best for us. How does he do that? He whispers bad thoughts in our minds.[114:4-6] When bad thoughts enter our minds and we listen to them, we are actually listening to Shaitān's words.

مِن شَرِّ ٱلۡوَسۡوَاسِ ٱلۡخَنَّاسِ ۝

ٱلَّذِى يُوَسۡوِسُ فِى صُدُورِ ٱلنَّاسِ ۝

مِنَ ٱلۡجِنَّةِ وَٱلنَّاسِ ۝

(Our Rabb, save us) from the evil of the whispering of the sneaking one, who whispers into the hearts of mankind, from among the jinn or the mankind. (114:4–6)

Shaitān's promise is false: In order to make us go down the wrong path, Shaitān makes false promises to us.[4:120; 14:22] He tells us to follow a certain path, but he would never say that the path is wrong. He will make us believe the path is good, and if we follow the path, we will have happiness or good things in life. If we do not listen to him, he will continue to offer tempting ideas. He will continue to try to make us believe that he is our good friend, and the path he is showing us is a good path.

Once he told prophet Adam (A) to eat the fruit from a tree in the Garden. Allāh had already told Adam (A) not to go near the tree.[7:19] Shaitān told Adam (A) that if he ate the fruit, he would become an angel or he might live forever.[7:20; 20:120] Shaitān pretended that he wanted good things for Adam (A), but actually he wanted to destroy him. Adam (A) listened to Shaitān and tasted the fruit from the tree.[7:22] After tasting it, Adam (A) did not become an angel nor did he live forever. Shaitān was successful in misleading Adam (A). Allāh punished Adam (A) for disobeying Him. Adam (A) was thrown out of the Garden.

Shaitān appears as a friend: Shaitān is our enemy, but he acts as if he is our friend. He makes us believe that the bad things are full of fun. He makes us believe that bad things will make us happy. He encourages us to go for it. For example, people who take drugs have become friends of Shaitān. People start to think that drugs will make them feel better or make them forget their sorrow. Shaitān promises that nothing will happen if a person takes drugs once in a while. He tells the person that nobody will find out. But once the person tries drugs, it leads to endless trouble. Ultimately the drugs destroy the person.

Shaitān is everywhere: Shaitān's only job is to mislead human beings. In order to do that, he waits for us on every path we take. He comes closer to us from our right, left, front, and back.[7:11] This means that he tempts us every moment, at every place, and from every direction.

What Shaitān cannot do: Shaitān appears very strong, but in reality he is not powerful at all. He cannot force anybody to do anything. All he does is talk nicely and give false promises. His control applies only to people who do not obey Allāh and do not follow the right path. In the Qur'ān, Allāh said Shaitān's activity does not work on righteous people.[15:42; 17:65] Even Shaitān, himself, said he will mislead everybody except the truly good people.[15:40] He has no control over the truly good people.

Who is to be blamed: We may think that Shaitān attracts us, so we should blame only him. If we listen to him and respond to his temptations, then we are equally responsible. The blame goes to both us and Shaitān. Shaitān said: *"Surely Allāh promised you the promise of truth; I promised you, but I broke it to you. And I had no authority over you, except that I called you and you responded to me; therefore do not blame me, but blame yourselves. I cannot rescue you, and you cannot rescue me."* (14:22).

What we can do: Allāh says that He will punish those who follow Shaitān. Shaitān wants to defeat us and destroy us. He does not want us to go to Heaven. We must try to avoid Shaitān.

What do we need to do to avoid him? We can avoid him by not letting bad thoughts linger in our minds. We cannot stop thoughts from entering, but we can push the thoughts out of our minds. We can avoid Shaitān by listening only to Allāh and the teachings of Prophet Muhammad (S). Whenever our mind tells us something is not right, we should not do it. Our parents and teachers are the best people who can show us the right path. Sometimes the right path seems boring and the wrong path appears very attractive. However, we should remember that the wrong path will destroy us. Shaitān follows the wrong path, but we should follow the path to Allāh.

1. How does Shaitān appear to us?

    A.   He appears as our enemy.
    B.   He appears as our friend.
    C.   He appears as a scary monster.
    D.   He appears as an animal.

2. What were the two false promises that Shaitān made to prophet Adam (A)?

    A. _____

    B. _____

3. Shaitān can mislead all types of people except one type. Who are the people that Shaitān cannot mislead?

_____

4. Shaitān can come close to us from certain directions. Which of the following choices is correct about the directions?

    A.   He comes to us only from the right direction.
    B.   He comes to us only from the left direction.
    C.   He comes to us only from above.
    D.   He comes to us from all directions.

5. Find the following words in the word search puzzle below:

SHAITAN, TEMPTATION, ADAM, RIGHT PATH, ENEMY, FRIEND, MISLEAD, DESTROY, WHISPER, HELL, HEAVEN

D	A	R	T	S	W	U	A	D	A	M
E	S	A	E	N	E	M	Y	I	W	F
S	H	E	A	V	E	N	G	S	F	R
T	A	B	S	P	T	H	E	L	L	I
R	I	G	H	T	P	A	T	H	P	E
O	T	E	M	P	T	A	T	I	O	N
Y	A	Y	O	M	I	S	L	E	A	D
A	N	W	H	I	S	P	E	R	M	E

Hūd (A): *Struggle to Guide the Misguided*

Objective of the Lesson:

Prophet Hūd (A) was an important prophet of Allāh. This lesson provides a short account of the prophet, his community, and his teachings. Students will learn why and how Allāh punished this community. What lessons can we learn from the life of Hūd (A)?

Long before many of the famous prophets, like Mūsā (A) or Ibrāhīm (A), there was a prophet named of Hūd (A). He was born several generations after prophet Nūh (A). In the Qur'ān, sūrah 11 is named after Hūd (A).

Place of his mission: Hūd (A) lived and worked in the southern region of present-day Yemen. The name of the region is **Hadramouth**. The Qur'ān says he lived in the city of **Iram**.[89:7] Archeological discoveries found a city named **Ubar** in the southern part of Arabia. The archeologists think that the lost city of Ubar was actually the city Iram mentioned in the Qur'ān.

Skill and success of 'Ad: As with all other prophets, Hūd (A) also worked among his people. The people of 'Ad were successful, powerful, and they could do uncommon things. For example, they built beautiful houses and tall structures on the mountains. They were great craftsmen, masha Allāh.

How did the people of 'Ad become so successful? They became

successful because they worked hard and Allāh rewarded them for their efforts. They were intelligent and used their intelligence in a good way. Their story proves that success comes from our efforts, but ultimately it is Allāh who gives us everything.

Pride corrupted 'Ad: As the people of 'Ad became wealthy, they started to become proud. Slowly they began to ignore the need to worship Allāh. They began to set up new gods to worship. They were skilled at carving out figures on the mountains. They began to treat some of these figures as replicas of their gods. Thus, they started idol-worshipping. Allāh sent Hūd (A) as a prophet to guide them to worship One Allāh. The leaders among the people of 'Ad laughed at Hūd (A). They told him: *We think you are a foolish person and we think you are telling lies.*[7:66]

Hūd (A) gave them good advice: Hūd (A) tried to make them understand that he was not foolish. He tried to show the people that he was a messenger of Allāh. The people of 'Ad could not understand why Allāh would send a human being as a prophet. Hūd (A) told them there was nothing strange about a human being becoming a prophet. He reminded them that Allāh's blessing was upon them.[7:69]

The people asked why should they worship Allāh when they cannot even see Him. They had become used to worshipping idols for a long time. Their forefathers also worshiped idols. They thought they were doing nothing wrong by worshipping idols. Hūd (A) tried to make them understand that the idols were useless things. The people of 'Ad probably thought Hūd (A) was trying to make some money. He told them: *I ask from you no reward for my teaching. My reward will come only from Him who created me.*[11:51]

Hūd (A) warned his people that they should ask for forgiveness from Allāh and repent to Him. Allāh might forgive them and give them abundant rain in this desert and make them more powerful.[11:52] A good rainfall would be a blessing to them. Even then the people of 'Ad did not listen. They thought some of their idol gods turned Hūd (A) into a crazy person. The people of 'Ad remained stubborn.

Hūd (A) reminded them that they would not live forever in the buildings they carved out on the mountains.[26:129] They would die one day, so it was important to be good and hope for a reward from Allāh. The people told Hūd (A) that they would not listen to him, no matter how much he tried. They believed Hūd's (A) warnings were false warnings. They thought that whatever Hūd (A) said was nothing but stories from the past.[26:136-137]

Punishment for disobedience of Allāh: Hūd (A) told them that if they did not listen to his good advice, Allāh might punish them. The leaders among the 'Ad still did not care. They challenged Hūd (A) to bring punishment upon them. They thought Hūd (A) was lying, and that no punishment would ever fall upon them.

Ultimately, when the people of 'Ad did not listen to the good advice and continued to worship the idols, Allāh punished them. They were destroyed by a fierce hurricane, or wind storm.[41:16; 54:19–20, 69:6–7] Allāh says:

We therefore sent on them a furious hurricane during unlucky days that We might make them taste a degrading chastisement in the present life. And surely the punishment of the Hereafter is more shameful; and they will not be helped. (41:16)

In the Qur'ān Allāh compares their destruction to uprooted date trees. Date trees are strong and their roots go deep under the ground. Ordinary storms can do little to the trees, however, the people of 'Ad were so severely destroyed, it was as if they were date trees plucked out of the ground and thrown away.[54:20]

Lesson for us: From the story of 'Ad, we learned the consequence of disobeying Allāh. If we disobey Allāh and ignore His commands, we may enjoy life for a while, just like the people of 'Ad. However, in the end, they were punished and destroyed. Similarly, unless we stay on the right path, we, too, may suffer punishment and destruction.

Interesting Facts

According to the current meteorological definition, a hurricane has a wind speed of more than 74 miles per hour (mph). Tropical storms have speeds of 39–73 mph. A tropical depression has speeds of less than 39 mph.

Depending on the location it occurs on earth, a hurricane is called a typhoon or a cyclone.

1. The Qur'ān mentions the city of prophet Hūd (A) and his people. What was the name of the city as mentioned in the Qur'ān?

_____

2. What types of houses did the people of 'Ad build?

_____

3. What types of gods did the people of 'Ad worship?

_____

4. Read the English translation of verse 7:68 in sūrah Al-A'rāf. Based on the verse, write the two things Hūd (A) told the people.

A. _____

B. _____

5. Read the English translation of verse 69:6 in sūrah Al-Hāqqah. How were the people of 'Ad destroyed?

_____

6. Fill in the blanks with the correct names.

Hūd (A) arrived several generations after prophet _____ and several generations before prophet _____ and prophet _____.

7. In which region did the people of 'Ad live?

    A.   North of Arabia in Syria.
    B.   South of Arabia in the Hadramouth region.
    C.   East of Baghdad in Iraq.
    D.   In northern Africa.

Sālih (A): *Struggle to Guide the Misguided*

Objective of the Lesson:

This lesson provides a short account of prophet Sālih (A) and his people. Students will learn how his people rejected their prophet and how Allāh punished them. Students will also learn the important moral lesson from the historical account.

In the previous lesson, we learned about prophet Hūd (A) and his people named 'Ad. After the people were destroyed, the tribe of Thamūd came into prominence. The tribe of Thamūd did not live in the same area where the people of Hūd (A) lived. The people of Thamūd lived in the northern part of present-day Saudi Arabia, near the **Madyan** region.

The two tribes: The tribes of 'Ad and Thamūd had several similarities between them. The Qur'ān sometimes mentions them in the same sūrah. Both tribes were very successful and prosperous at the time.

They achieved power and glory that were uncommon at that time. Both tribes knew how to build tall buildings on the plains and how to carve out beautiful homes in the mountains. After they reached their glory days, both tribes started idol-worshipping. Most of the idols were carved out of rocks. Over time the people became proud and cruel.

Teachings of Sālih (A): To the Thamūd tribe, Allāh sent prophet Sālih (A), who was from their own community. The Qur'ān mentions him as a "brother" because he was not a stranger to them.[27:45] Earlier, people used to respect him. When he began teaching the Oneness of Allāh, the same people became angry with him. He told them:

$$\text{قَالَ يَٰقَوْمِ ٱعْبُدُواْ ٱللَّهَ مَا لَكُم مِّنْ إِلَٰهٍ غَيْرُهُۥ ۖ هُوَ أَنشَأَكُم مِّنَ ٱلْأَرْضِ}$$

$$\text{وَٱسْتَعْمَرَكُمْ فِيهَا فَٱسْتَغْفِرُوهُ ثُمَّ تُوبُوٓاْ إِلَيْهِ ۚ إِنَّ رَبِّى قَرِيبٌ مُّجِيبٌ ۝}$$

O my people! worship Allāh, you have no deity other than Him. He evolved you from the earth and settled you in it; therefore ask forgiveness of Him, and then turn towards Him. Surely my Rabb is very Near, most Responsive. (11:61)

Unfortunately, the people did not want to give up their old ways.[11:62]

People demanded a sign: The people could not believe how Sālih (A) could be a prophet. To them he was just a simple man. They did not care to understand his message. They worshipped idols as their gods. Their forefathers worshipped idols and they blindly followed their forefathers. They demanded that if Sālih (A) was speaking the truth, he should bring a sign. Sālih (A) brought a she-camel as a sign for the people. The people were not happy with this sign. They continued idol-worshipping.

She-camel as a sign: The Qurʾān does not say anything about how the she-camel was selected. There are a number of ancient stories about the miraculous nature of the she-camel. Most of the stories say a rock in the mountain split open and a camel came out of the rock.

Hatred towards the camel: The people of Thamūd initially disliked Sālih (A). After the she-camel was provided as a sign, people began to hate the she-camel. They started to complain that the she-camel drank all the water from their well. They began to make secret plots to harm the camel. When Sālih (A) learned about these plans, he said:

$$\text{وَيَٰقَوْمِ هَٰذِهِۦ نَاقَةُ ٱللَّهِ لَكُمْ ءَايَةً فَذَرُوهَا تَأْكُلْ فِىٓ أَرْضِ}$$

$$\text{ٱللَّهِ وَلَا تَمَسُّوهَا بِسُوٓءٍ فَيَأْخُذَكُمْ عَذَابٌ قَرِيبٌ ۝}$$

O my people! this is the she-camel of Allāh, a Sign for you; so leave her to pasture in Allāh's earth, and do not touch her with evil, lest an imminent punishment should overtake you. (11:64)

People hurt the camel: The people of Thamūd did not listen to Sālih (A). One day they injured the camel by cutting the hamstring of her leg. A hamstring is the large tendon in the back of the legs. The camel could not walk anymore, therefore she could not search for food or drink water. Eventually the large camel died of starvation. It was a merciless method of killing an innocent animal.

Sālih (A) warns of punishment: After the camel was killed, Sālih (A) told the people of Thamūd that their punishment would come within three days. But the people laughed and challenged Sālih (A) to bring the punishment immediately. They thought no punishment would fall upon them.

Plot against Sālih (A): In the meantime, the tribe also made a secret plot to kill Sālih (A). Nine people from the tribe decided to kill Sālih (A), and then tell the people later that they had nothing to do with his death.[7:49] But Allāh saved him from their secret plot.

Punishment arrives: Due to the severity of their cruelty and rejection of the messenger, Allāh sent a severe punishment. The people of Thamūd were destroyed by a severe earthquake. It caused a loud, thundering noise. Everyone died and their homes were leveled to dust.[41:17; 69:5]

Lessons for us: How does the history of Thamūd apply to us today? We too are a technologically superior race. We have tremendous amounts of knowledge, skills and abilities. Also, we are a prosperous nation. We also build magnificent buildings. Now, after all these advancements, if we disobey Allāh and reject the message of our Messenger (S), do you think Allāh will accept our conduct? Why does the Qur'ān tell us the stories of 'Ad and Thamūd? Obviously, the purpose is to warn us about our own conduct.

If we disobey Allāh and ignore His commands, we may enjoy life for a while. The people of 'Ad and Thamūd enjoyed life for a while. But in the end, they were punished and destroyed. Similarly, unless we stay on the right path, we may also suffer punishment and destruction.

1. What is the name of the region where the people of Thamūd lived?

_____

2. What types of houses did the people of Thamūd build?

_____

3. The people of Thamūd had many similarities with the people of 'Ad. Which choice below about their similarities is correct?

    A.   They used to worship camels.
    B.   They used to build tall buildings carved out of rock.
    C.   They used to follow their prophets.
    D.   They used to worship idols.

4. How did the people of Thamūd kill the she-camel that was provided as a sign to them?

    A.   They killed her in front of the idols.
    B.   They pushed her down the mountain slope.
    C.   They shot her with bows and arrows.
    D.   They cut her leg.

5. Read verse 7:78. How were their houses destroyed?

_____

6. After the people of Thamūd injured or hamstrung the she-camel, how many days later did the punishment arrive? Read verse 11:65 to find the answer.

_____

Mūsā (A): *His Life and Achievements*

Objective of the Lesson:

This lesson provides a summary of the life and achievements of prophet Mūsā (A). Students will learn about his early life, his life in Egypt and Madyan, and again in Egypt. Students will also learn about the interaction of Mūsā (A) with the Children of Israel.

Mūsā (A) was one of the most important prophets in Islam. He lived about 3,000 years ago. The Children of Israel consider him their most prominent prophet. The Divine book named **Tawrat** was revealed to him. Jewish people follow the guidance contained in the Tawrat.

In this lesson, we will learn about the life and achievements of Mūsā (A). His entire life is very eventful. The Qur'ān describes his early childhood and adult life in many sūrahs.

Early childhood: There was a time when Fir'awn tortured the Israelites in Egypt. He ordered all the newborn Israelite male children to be killed and to let the female children live.[2:49] When Mūsā (A) was born, his mother was afraid for his life. She knew Fir'awn's people would soon come to kill her child. Allāh wanted to save Mūsā (A). He revealed to Mūsā's mother to place him in a basket in the river.[28:7]

Mūsā's mother placed her child in a basket and it floated on the river. The basket continued to float in the river. It so happened that the basket reached the palace of Fir'awn. Fir'awn's wife picked up the basket and the child. She said she would adopt the child as their son. Now no one could kill the baby.

At the palace, infant Mūsā (A) continued to cry.[28:12] Mūsā's sister had followed the basket. She arrived at the palace and told them she could find a woman who would feed the baby. She did not disclose her identity or the identity of the woman who would feed him. Then she brought her own mother. She,

too, did not disclose her identity. Infant Mūsā (A) liked her—and why not? She was, after all, his own mother. Thus, the mother was reunited with her son and she was able to feed him.[28:13]

Mūsā (A) began a new life in Fir'awn's palace as his adopted son—in a princely manner. He began receiving all the good things in life. This is how Allāh prepared him to assume greater roles in the future.

Street fight: When Mūsā (A) was a young man, he noticed an Israelite and an Egyptian fighting on the street. He tried to solve their problem. To stop them from fighting, he struck the Egyptian. The Egyptian died from the strike. Mūsā (A) was very sorry for the incident and asked for forgiveness from Allāh. For this accident, Fir'awn wanted to punish Mūsā (A) with death. Mūsā (A) realized that he would not receive justice in Egypt, so he ran away. After traveling in the desert for many days, he reached a place called **Madyan**.

Life in Madyan: In Madyan, Mūsā (A) met a family. The elderly man of the family asked Mūsā (A) to marry one of his daughters and stay with them for eight to ten years. Mūsā (A) then started a family in Madyan. One day, while he was traveling with his family, he noticed a fire on a mountain. He went to the mountain, hoping to receive guidance. There he received instructions from Allāh to go back to Egypt and Fir'awn. His mission would be to lead Fir'awn to the right path and rescue the Israelites. At that time Allāh gave him two signs—(1) when he threw his rod, it would turn into a snake, and (2) when he drew his hand from his chest, it would turn white. Mūsā (A) asked Allāh to let his brother, Hārūn (A), travel with him because Hārūn (A) was a good speaker.

Mūsā (A) returns to Egypt: In Egypt, Mūsā (A) asked the people to give up idol-worshipping and obey Allāh. Fir'awn laughed at him. He did not believe Mūsā (A) was a prophet. He asked him to show proof. Mūsā (A) threw his rod and it became a snake. He drew his hand from his chest and it appeared white. Firʿawn thought it was only a magic trick. He challenged Mūsā (A) and said that his own magicians could perform better magic.

Magicians challenges Mūsā (A): Firʿawn arranged a festival to defeat Mūsā (A). He invited all of the important magicians from different parts of the country. The magicians came, hoping to defeat Mūsā (A) and receive a reward from Firʿawn. When the magicians threw their rods, they became snakes. It was a terrifying sight. But when Mūsā (A) threw his rod, it began to eat what they created out of magic. Seeing this, the magicians realized that Mūsā (A) was speaking the truth. They bowed down on the ground and believed in One Allāh.[7:120–121] This made Firʿawn even angrier. He threatened to punish the magicians.

Rescue of the Israelites: Mūsā (A) lived in Egypt for a few more years. Firʿawn did not listen to Mūsā's (A) teachings. Finally, Allāh instructed Mūsā (A) to rescue the Israelites. Mūsā (A) took them across the sea on the other side of Egypt. Firʿawn needed these people to work as laborers. To stop them from escaping from Egypt, he chased them. Before Firʿawn could catch them, Mūsā (A) and his people had already crossed the sea. Firʿawn followed them in the sea, thinking that he could cross it like the Israelites did earlier. By the time he reached the middle of the sea, the water came from all sides and drowned him.[10:90]

Life after rescue: After Mūsā (A) rescued the Israelites, he went to Mount Sinai to meditate and receive further guidance from Allāh. During his absence, the Israelites made a golden cow and began to worship it. When Mūsā (A) returned, he was very angry with the people.[2:54] He made them destroy the golden cow and start worshipping Allāh again.

The Israelites continued to annoy Mūsā (A) with their rebellious activities. They did not follow his instructions properly, and they did many things that made him angry. Mūsā (A) wanted them to occupy the Promised Land, but they refused because they were scared of death.

The Israelites remained in the wilderness for 40 long years.[5:26] Life became very difficult for them. During this period, Mūsā (A) passed away. Allāh wanted to help and bless them, but they refused to follow Allāh's guidance.

1. Name the place where Mūsā (A) was married.

   _____

2. When infant Mūsā (A) was crying, who helped the queen to find a woman to feed him?

   _____

3. When Mūsā (A) was a young man, he accidentally killed a person. Who was the person?

   A. The king's nephew.
   B. An Egyptian.
   C. An Israelite.
   D. A traveler who needed money.

4. What were the two signs Allāh gave to Mūsā (A) before Mūsā (A) returned to Egypt?

   1) _____

   2) _____

5. Using an English translation of the Qur'ān, read verse 20:70. Who fell down on the ground and believed in Allāh?

   _____

6. Read verse 20:71. Fir'awn threatened to punish the magicians in a brutal manner. What did he say he would do to the magicians?

   1) _____

   2) _____

7. Relate the message of verse 20:71 to verses 7:123–124. What is the overall message of these verses?

   _____

Sulaimān (A): *A King and A Servant of Allāh*

Objective of the Lesson:

This lesson provides a brief account of prophet Sulaimān (A). The Qur'ān talks about his wealth, power, and righteousness. Students will learn about his achievements and interaction with the queen of Sheba.

About 3,000 years ago, Prophet Sulaimān (A) lived in ancient Palestine. He was the richest prophet and a king. Many legends are narrated about his life. He had extraordinary power and wisdom. He was an excellent judge. The Qur'ān mentions some examples of his judgment.[21:78–79]

Sulaimān's ancestors: His father, Dāwūd (A), was also a prophet and a king. His ancestor was Ibrāhīm (A). Ibrāhīm (A) had two sons, Ismā'īl (A) and Ishāq (A). Sulaimān (A) was a descendant of Ishāq (A). "Descendant" means someone born from a family member who lived long ago. Prophet Dāwūd (A) had several children. Among them, Sulaimān (A) was the wisest and most righteous. He was close to his father.

Sulaimān's kingdom: When Dāwūd (A) passed away, Sulaimān (A) was the best person to inherit the kingdom. He prayed to Allāh to give him such a kingdom that nobody else could have after him. Allāh granted his prayer and gave him the best kingdom at that time. Also, in response to Sulaimān's prayer,

Allāh made sure no one could have a kingdom as good as Sulaimān's (A) kingdom.

Sulaimān's power and army: Sulaimān (A) had a large army to run his vast kingdom. His army included horses, camels, birds, and jinn. He also had a large number of ships that were used to conquer other territories and do business in far-off places. His ships used the power of wind for his benefit. He also had the ability to understand the language and behavior of birds and animals. He used skillful builders to construct palaces for him. The jinn dove for him under the sea to extract pearls.

Sulaimān's judgment: Sulaimān was known as a good judge. Everybody liked his keen sense of judgment. One day, two people came to him with a problem. One of them owned a field of crops and the other owned sheep. One night the sheep entered the field and destroyed the crops.[21:78] Sulaimān's judgment made both parties happy.[21:79] There is also a legend about Sulaimān (A) judging the case of a lost child. Two women claimed that they were the mother of the same child. Sulaimān (A) suggested cutting the child in two halves and give one half to each mother. On hearing this, the actual mother cried out not to cut the baby. Sulaimān (A) realized that this woman was the actual mother. He handed the child over to the actual mother.

Sulaimān and the queen of Sheba: Sulaimān (A) learned about the kingdom of Sheba and its queen. The queen's name was Bilqis. The country was very rich and it had all the wealth that a person could dream of. But the queen worshipped the sun instead of Allāh. When Sulaimān (A) found out about this, he sent a letter to the queen asking her to accept Islam. The queen sent him a costly gift. Sulaimān (A) did not want the gift because Allāh gave him everything he needed in this world.[27:36] He sent the gift back and informed the

queen that if she did not submit to Allāh, he would come and conquer her land.

Queen Bilqis decided to meet Sulaimān (A) personally. She thought that by visiting him, she could prevent him from attacking her country. When she left her city to meet Sulaimān (A), he arranged to secretly bring her throne to his palace. He ordered his people to change the throne to test Bilqis. When the queen saw it, she said she would love to have a throne just like this throne, not realizing that it was her throne.

Later Bilqis entered the palace. The palace had glass slabs on the floor and under the glass slabs water was flowing. From a distance it looked like the entire floor was full of water. The queen did not realize the glass slabs were there. When she stepped inside the palace, she lifted her skirt slightly so as not to get it wet. Then she realized the water was underneath the glass slabs.[27:44] This made her understand that all her life, she was searching for false happiness, leaving out actual happiness. Actual happiness comes from Allāh. Then she accepted Islam.

Sulaimān's death: After Sulaimān (A) passed away, the kingdom broke up into several parts because his sons were not good rulers.

1. Name Sulaimān's three famous ancestors, who were also prophets of Allāh.

    1)   _____

    2)   _____

    3)   _____

2. Which country did Sulaimān (A) want to occupy unless its ruler accepted Islam?

    A.   Egypt.
    B.   Syria.
    C.   Sheba.
    D.   Sinai Peninsula.

3. Using an English translation of the Qur'an, read verse 27:15. What did Allāh give to both Dāwūd (A) and Sulaimān (A)?

_____

4. When Sulaimān (A) became a king, he prayed to Allāh for a special type of kingdom. What type of kingdom did he want?

_____

5. What happened to Sulaimān's (A) kingdom after his death?

_____

Truthfulness: *An Important Quality for Muslims*

Objective of the Lesson:

In our everyday lives, we have to uphold the truth at all costs. Rasūlullāh (S) always encouraged people to uphold the truth. This lesson discusses why truthfulness is an important quality we should aim to uphold.

If we ask people what they mean by truthfulness, the most common answer would be to speak the truth. This is a correct answer, but it is not the complete answer. Truthfulness is the total character of a person. It is an identifying mark of a Muslim. It shows what the person is, outwardly and inwardly—in his speech, conduct, and dealings with people. If you only speak the truth but do not develop truthfulness in your conduct and dealings with people, you cannot be truthful. Our Nabi Muhammad (S) always spoke the truth. He never lied, and he showed truthfulness in his behavior.

Allāh created the heavens and the earth with Truth. He requires people to base their lives on truth, to speak the truth, to act with truth, and to believe in nothing but the truth. If we do not follow and live by truth, we will be in trouble. If we are truthful in life, we will receive a great

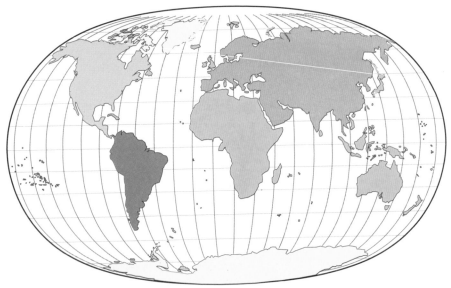

benefit on the Day of Judgment. Allāh says that the most successful people will be those who are truthful. For them, Allāh has kept Paradise, and Allāh will be happy with them.[5:119]

This is the Day on which their truthfulness will benefit the truthful. For them are Gardens beneath which flow the rivers, abiding in it all the time. Allāh is well-pleased with them and they are well-pleased with Him. This is the great achievement. (5:119)

Rasūlullāh (S) was truthful: Even before Muhammad (S) became a nabi of Allāh, people knew him as a truthful person. People in Makkah called him **As-Sadiq** (truthful) and **Al-Amin** (trustworthy). They never heard him speak a single lie. Because of his truthful nature, he earned the trust of the people. However, when the Qur'ān was revealed, people did not listen to Muhammad (S), thinking that he was making up stories. It did not take long before everybody was convinced of the truth. If Muhammad (S) had ever told a lie, Islam would not have spread.

Example from a hadīth: It is reported that a man came to Nabi Muhammad (S) and confessed that he was addicted to many bad things, such as theft, lying, drinking, and so on. He wanted to correct himself. He asked Rasūlullāh (S) to tell him one bad habit to give up first. Rasūlullāh (S) told him to give up lying. The man promised that he would never tell a lie. During the night, he was about to drink alcohol. Suddenly it occurred to him that if Rasūlullāh (S) asked him what was he doing, he would have to tell the truth or lie about it. But he could not lie. This thought made him stay away from drinking. Next, he was going to steal in the darkness of the night. Again, the thought of telling Rasūlullāh  (S) the truth or lie about it kept him from stealing. Similarly, he could not commit any other sin for fear of lying. The next morning, he went to Rasūlullāh (S) and told him that he was able to stay away from all the sins simply by avoiding lies.

Every prophet was truthful: The Qur'ān mentions Ibrāhīm (A) was a truthful person.[19:41] His son Ismā'īl (A) was a man of his word, which means he always kept his word, he was truthful.[19:54] Another prophet named Idrīs (A) was also truthful.[19:56] Prophet Yūsuf (A) was truthful.[12:46] Maryam, mother of 'Isā (A), was a truthful woman.[5:75] In fact, truthfulness was the main quality of every single prophet. Rasūlullāh (S) gave Abū Bakr (r) the title **as-Siddiq**, which means "the truthful one." This title was given to him because Abū Bakr was a truthful person in his faith and in his dealings.

Practice being truthful: We cannot become truthful in one day. We have to practice truthfulness. We can start by making sure we speak the truth. Sometimes truth may bring hardship. But remember, if you are truthful, Allāh will help you. Your hardship will go away. Rasūlullāh (S) was always truthful, even when he faced difficulties in life. But he never compromised with the truth—that is, he never mixed truth with falsehood. Soon his difficulties were over and he continued to receive Allāh's blessings and rewards.

Truthfulness is not just speaking the truth, but behaving in a truthful manner. If someone trusts us not to spread a secret, we should keep the secret. If someone trusts us to keep an item safely, we should take care of it and return it when they ask for it. If we promise something we must keep the promise.

Truthfulness leads to forgiveness: If we are truthful, we can expect forgiveness from Allāh. Our truthfulness will benefit us on the Day of Judgment as well. By practicing truthfulness, a person becomes better in the sight of Allāh. A truthful person is a righteous person. We must fear Allāh and always tell the truth. If we lie, it will create serious problems for us in the Hereafter. If we die without asking Allāh's forgiveness and we are recorded as liars, then we will have a terrible punishment in the Hereafter. We must try our best not to lie.

Reward of being truthful: The greatest reward for being truthful in life is forgiveness and Paradise. In sūrah al-Ahzāb Allāh says He has prepared forgiveness and a great reward for truthful men and truthful women.[33:35]

Points to Ponder
In addition to speaking the truth, what are several other ways we can be truthful? What are some of the rewards mentioned in the Qur'ān for being truthful?

from hadith

It is related by Bukhari, Muslim, Abu Dawūd, and Tirmidhi that Rasūlullāh (S) said: "Maintain truthfulness, for truthfulness leads to righteousness, and righteousness leads to Heaven. A man continues to maintain truthfulness until he is recorded in Allāh's book as truthful. Refrain from lying, because lying leads to blatant evil, and evil leads to the Fire. A man continues to lie until he is recorded in Allāh's book as a liar."

1. Which of the following choices is correct about the complete meaning of truthfulness?

    A.   It is only about telling the truth.
    B.   It is about behaving in a truthful manner.
    C.   It is only about keeping the trust of other people.
    D.   It is only about doing good deeds.

2. Read verse 19:41. What does the verse say about the conduct of Prophet Ibrāhīm (A)?

_____

3. When the truth is revealed, something happens and it always happens. Read verse 17:81 to answer what happens after the truth comes out.

_____

4. In verse 2:42, Allāh says not to do something with the Truth. Read the verse and write what He tells us not to do with the Truth.

_____

5. Write two titles people lovingly gave to Muhammad (S) for being truthful.

    1) _____

    2) _____

Perseverance: *Keep on Trying*

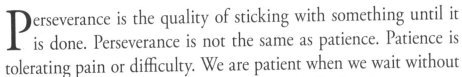

Objective of the Lesson:

Using the examples of Dāwūd (A) and Muhammad (S), students will learn how to achieve success. One of the ways to achieve success is through perseverance. Students will memorize a du'ā made by Dāwūd (A) when he faced this ferocious enemy, Jālūt.

Perseverance is the quality of sticking with something until it is done. Perseverance is not the same as patience. Patience is tolerating pain or difficulty. We are patient when we wait without complaining until the difficulty disappears or gets better by itself. When we persevere, we work hard to remove our difficulty. Perseverance is patience together with constant work to remove the problem. Climbing a mountain is an act of perseverance. Unless we work hard to climb, we will not reach the top of the mountain. When we continue to work hard, it means we stick with our project and become successful.

The Arabic word for perseverance is *sabr*. In sūrah Al-'Asr, Allāh (swt) tells us that one of the strongest qualities of successful people is sabr.[103:3] Sometimes Allāh (swt) tests us with fear, hunger, loss of property, and lives. However, those who persevere receive glad tidings or good news of rewards from Allāh (swt).[2:155] Allāh (swt) told us to be patient and to be even better at persevering.[3:200]

Sometimes it seems that our efforts are too weak to complete a project. If you have to cut down a large tree, two or three strokes of an ax will hardly do the job. This will only chip small chunks of wood. If you persevere and continue striking the tree, it will not be long before the tree falls down. Every project may appear as big as an oak tree, and our efforts as small as an ax. Still if we are persistent, we can accomplish any big task.

Long ago, there was a giant named Jālūt (Goliath). He was big, tough, and ruthless. Nobody could fight him. Everybody gave up the plan to stop him from his evil actions. There was a young boy named Dāwūd (A) who did not give up. He persevered and kept on trying. Dāwūd (A) and Tālūt (Saul) arrived with a small army to fight Jālūt. They asked Allāh (swt) to give them perseverance. They prayed:

رَبَّنَآ أَفْرِغْ عَلَيْنَا صَبْرًا وَثَبِّتْ أَقْدَامَنَا وَٱنصُرْنَا عَلَى ٱلْقَوْمِ ٱلْكَـٰفِرِينَ ۝

Rabbanā afrigh 'alaynā sabran wa thabbit aqdāmanā wa-nsurnā 'ala-l qawmi-l kāfirīn.

Our Rabb! Pour down upon us perseverance, and make our feet firm, and help us against the unbelieving people. (2:250)

Dāwūd (A) and Tālūt had persevered, therefore they were able to defeat the mighty Jālūt. Dāwūd (A) was a young boy when he defeated Jālūt. We learn from this event that it is not size or age that matters; it is perseverance that makes the difference.

Our Nabi Muhammad (S) was tortured and attacked by nonbelievers. How did he become so successful against the nonbelievers? By the grace of Allāh (swt), our Rasūl (S) practiced perseverance and persisted in his mission. He tried telling the idol-worshippers of Makkah to be good and to follow the path of Allāh (swt). Many people would not listen to him; but this did not discourage our Rasūl (S). He did not give up. He kept on trying. He had to move to Madinah to keep teaching people. In many places in the Qur'ān, Allāh (swt) advises him: *"Therefore you do persevere; surely the promise of Allāh is true."* [30:60, 40:55, 77]

Sometimes it seems that sticking to a plan is difficult. Sometimes the plan itself seems difficult. No matter how difficult the plan is, having confidence is the first step of having perseverance. If we continue to show perseverance, it will finally produce results. Think of any world-famous athlete and you will find that the key to their success is perseverance. They did not become famous in one day. It took lots of perseverance and dedication. When one attains success in smaller things, his or her confidence increases and the person shows more perseverance to do even better. The power of perseverance is more magical and rewarding than one could ever imagine. All we have to do is start taking small steps.

Fasting during Ramadan teaches us how to stick to a plan, even if there is hardship. If we can tolerate hunger and thirst, we can manage many other difficulties with equal ease. The meal after a fast tastes good, and success after continuous effort is also very pleasing.

Whether you are solving a difficult math problem, drawing a picture, or working on a science project, you will be successful if you persevere. Many people do not achieve success because they give up before reaching the goal. Allāh (swt) advises us to be persistent in reaching success. Certainly, the advice of Allāh (swt) is the best. Allāh (swt) always helps those who try. [8:46]

from**hadith**

It is narrated that Rasūlullāh (S) said: "Surely, a great reward comes from a great trial: When Allāh (swt) loves a people, He puts them on trial. He who accepts the trial will enjoy Allāh's pleasure, and he who is unhappy with it will have Allāh's displeasure."

1. What is the difference between patience and perseverance?

   _____

   _____

   _____

   _____.

2. Memorize the du'ā that Dāwūd (A) made when he faced Jālūt. Be prepared to recite the du'ā in front of your teacher.

3. What quality did Dāwūd (A) have that gave him victory over Jālūt?

   _____

4. Read the English translation of sūrah Al-Insān, verse 76:12. How will Allāh (swt) reward those who persevere, or those who have patience and work hard?

   _____

5. Read sūrah 39, verse 10. What will be the limit of the reward for those who persevere?

   _____

   _____

6. Write two things that Rasūlullāh (S) did when the people of Makkah did not listen to him.

   1) _____

   2) _____

Day of Judgment: *The Day of Ultimate Justice*

Objective of the Lesson:

The Day of Judgment is a reality from which none of us can escape. When will it happen and what happens on that day? This lesson provides a short summary about the Day of Judgment.

In this lesson, we will learn about the Day of Judgment. The Day of Judgment will happen on *yawm al-qiyāmah*. The word *yawm* means "day," and *al-qiyāmah* means "**the resurrection**." Resurrection means to come back to life after death. On the Day of Judgment, all people will be either rewarded or punished by Allāh according to their beliefs and deeds. Those who do good deeds in this life will be rewarded on the Day of Judgment. Those who do the wrong things in this life be punished on the Day of Judgment.

Other names for the Day of Judgment: The Qur'ān mentions the Day of Judgment by many other names. The Day of Resurrection is the main name. But it is also known as the Awakening, the Hour, the Day of Account, the Day of Gathering, the Day of Distress, and the Day of Calculation. Each name indicates one special aspect about that day.

When it will happen: The Day of Judgment will happen in the future. Only Allāh knows when it will happen. We do not know the date or time of the Day. As Muslims we must believe in the Day of Judgment. Belief in the Day of Judgment is part of our Iman, or faith. The Qur'ān talks about the Day of Judgment in many sūrahs. It will happen when people are not at all prepared. It will happen all of a sudden. When Allāh decides it will happen, He will tell angel Israfil to blow a trumpet.[6:73] He will blow it and the Day of Judgment will begin.

Why the Day of Judgment: The main reason for the Day of Judgment is to provide justice. Many times in this world, a sinner is not punished in his lifetime. We also see good believers suffering in poverty or other difficulties. Sometimes justice happens in this life, but many times we cannot see how it happened. Sometimes justice happens long after we die. All these are principles of Allāh. The Day of Judgment is set so that absolute justice is provided to each and every person.

On that day, the smallest of our good deeds or bad actions will be brought before us and we will be held responsible. We will be judged based on each and every action. Nobody can escape from justice. On that day, justice will not be delayed or denied, but will be provided with absolute fairness. Every good deed will be rewarded, and every bad deed will be punished.

Examples of good and bad actions: The Day of Judgment is essential to keeping balance in human conduct. Bad people must be punished and good people must be rewarded. Sometimes bad people escape human justice in this life because of their power and influence. However, they deserve punishment. Fir'awn must be punished and Mūsā (A) must be rewarded. Fir'awn tortured thousands of Israelites and killed their male children. These people did not receive justice in this world. Prophet 'Isa (A) was tortured by his own people, and justice was not served. These people must face judgment. Many good people die without receiving justice in this life. They deserve justice and a reward.

How we are going to be judged: In order to be judged correctly and accurately, our record has to be available. The record has to be accurate. In this life, whatever we do or don't do is being recorded for Allāh. On the Day of Judgment, He will show us our records. It will be like a video of our every action. Allāh says:

$$وَنُخْرِجُ لَهُۥ يَوْمَ ٱلْقِيَٰمَةِ كِتَٰبًا يَلْقَىٰهُ مَنشُورًا ۝$$

$$ٱقْرَأْ كِتَٰبَكَ كَفَىٰ بِنَفْسِكَ ٱلْيَوْمَ عَلَيْكَ حَسِيبًا ۝$$

On the Day of Judgment we shall bring out for him a scroll, which he will see spread open. Read your record. You, yourself, are sufficient as a witness against you this Day. (17:13–14)

Who will provide evidence: In any legal judgment, we need a witness. The judge will look at the witness and listen to his or her testimony. On the Day of Judgment, Allāh will produce witnesses and make us listen to their testimony. Everybody's activities are being recorded during their lifetime. It is a very accurate record. These records will be produced for us. We will not be able to deny the truth, because it will be so clear to us. Our limbs, tongues, and skin will bear witness against us.

What we can do now: The Day of Judgment is certain to happen. Nobody can escape this day. But we can prepare ourselves to face the Day of Judgment. People who live a righteous life on earth will have no fear on the Day of Judgment. Righteous people will be rewarded on the Day of Judgment. Only sinners will be punished. Therefore, we should prepare ourselves by always doing good deeds. We should perform salāt on time, pray to Allāh, fast in the month of Ramadan, give to charity and do all types of good deeds that Allāh likes. If we continue to be good people, we will have no fear on the Day of Judgment—we will be successful in the life to come after the Judgment.

	Points to Ponder
	The Day of Judgment is certain to happen. Yet, why do so many people remain unmindful of it?
	What are some of the ways a person can prepare to be rewarded on the Day of Judgment.

1. What is the main purpose of the Day of Judgment?

_____

2. Using an English translation of the Qur'ān, read sūrah Al-An'ām, verse 36. On the Day of Judgment, what will happen to those people who are already dead?

_____ .

3. What is not possible on the Day of Judgment? Circle the correct answer.

    A.   Some people will escape from judgment.
    B.   Judgment will be on time.
    C.   Judgment will be absolutely fair.
    D.   Every action will be accounted for.

4. In order to be successful on the Day of Judgment, what can we do now? Circle all the correct answers.

    A.   We can study hard.
    B.   We can start living a righteous life.
    C.   We can follow the Qur'ān and the Sunnah.
    D.   We can commit small sins but not big sins.
    E.   We can do good deeds.
    F.   We can fast in the month of Ramadan.

5. Circle T if the sentence is true. Circle F if the sentence is false.

The Day of Judgment will happen suddenly.	T	F
Rasūlullāh (S) will decide when the Day of Judgment should happen.	T	F
Angel Israfil will blow a trumpet to begin the Day of Judgment.	T	F
Our limbs, tongues, and skin will bear witness against us.	T	F

'Eid: *Significance of the Festivities*

Objective of the Lesson:

Muslims have two major festivals, Eid al-Fitr and Eid al-Adha. This lesson discusses the importance of the two Eids and when, in a calendar year, we celebrate Eid.

Muslims all over the world celebrate two festivals. These are Eid al-Fitr and Eid al-Adha. In this lesson, we will learn the significance of both Eids.

The Eid festivals are based on the Muslim calendar. Unlike the English calendar, which is based on the movement of the sun, the Muslim calendar is based on the movement of the moon. Therefore, the Muslim calendar is called a **lunar calendar**, and the English calendar is called a solar calendar. The Muslim calendar begins with the date of migration of Rasūlullāh (S) from Makkah to Madinah in the year 622 C.E.

Eid al-Fitr: Eid al-Fitr is celebrated at the end of the month of **Ramadan**. The month of Ramadan is the ninth month of the Muslim calendar. Eid al-Fitr is celebrated on the first day of the tenth month, **Shawwal**. To make it easy for everybody to celebrate the festival, Eid al-Fitr can be celebrated on any of the first three days of Shawwal.

The meaning of the word *Eid* is "festival." The meaning of *fitr* is "breaking." Therefore, Eid al-Fitr means the festival of breaking fast. In the month of Ramadan, all Muslims fast for 29 to 30 days. Although they break the fast every day, at the end of Ramadan, a festival is observed to mark the end of month-long fasting.

Eid al-Fitr is truly a day of great celebration. On that day, people gather for Eid prayer. This prayer is not compulsory, therefore it is called **wajib**. A wajib prayer means it is necessary and highly recommended. You may not miss it intentionally.

On this day, people visit friends and greet each other. Many people exchange gifts. Children wear new clothes. People also visit the graves of their dear ones to remember them and pray to Allāh to forgive them.

Eid al-Adha: The festival of Eid al-Adha is observed in the month of **Dhul-Hajj**. The meaning of Eid al-Adha is Festival of Sacrifice. This festival is observed soon after the Hajj, on the tenth day of Dhul Hajj, the last month of the Muslim calendar.

The festival of Eid al-Adha is observed to remember the sacrifice of prophet Ibrāhīm (A). He had a dream that he was sacrificing his first son Ismā'īl. When he told the dream to his son, his son replied that he was ready to lay down his life. Both father and son prepared for the sacrifice. Allāh wanted to see if they were ready to give up the dearest thing—life—for the sake of Allāh. Their intention was sincere. Therefore, Allāh told them that their intention was fulfilled. They were asked to sacrifice an animal instead.

On the day of Eid al-Adha, Muslims sacrifice animals, such as sheep, goats, cows or camels. The animal has to be a mammal. A bird cannot be sacrificed. The meat of the sacrificed animal is mostly given away to friends, relatives, and the needy.

Islamic Calendar Months			
Muharram	Safar	Rabi' al-awwal	Rabi' al-thani
Jumada al-awwal	Jumada al-thani	Rajab	Sha'aban
Ramadan	Shawwal	Dhu al-Qi'dah	Dhu al-Hijjah

This Eid celebration teaches us to be ready to sacrifice anything for the sake of Allāh. Ibrāhīm (A) loved his son very much, but he was ready to sacrifice him. Allāh does not want us to sacrifice our dear ones. All He wants is for us to be ready to sacrifice anything of value in our life. Such sacrifice should be offered in order to establish truth or to support any noble cause that pleases Allāh.

1. The Muslim calendar begins with the date of a certain event. What was the event?

_____

2. In which month is Eid al-Fitr observed?

    A.   Muharram.
    B.   Ramadan.
    C.   Shawwal.
    D.   Dhul Hajj.

3. In which month is Eid al-Adha celebrated?

    A.   Muharram.
    B.   Ramadan.
    C.   Shawwal.
    D.   Dhul Hajj.

4. Which Eid is celebrated in memory of Ibrāhīm's (A) willingness to sacrifice his son?

_____

5. What is the meaning of Eid al-Fitr?

    A.   Festival of sacrifice.
    B.   Festival of breaking fast.
    C.   Festival of the new moon.
    D.   Festival of exchanging gifts.

Appendix
Steps of Salāt

Physical preparation for salāh:

Physical cleanliness: Before performing salāh, make sure you have a clean body. You must complete *wudu*, and be in the state of *wudu*. At any time during the salāh, do not look sideways, do not look at others and do not talk to others during the salāh. Do not make unnecessary movements. Do not scratch, yawn, laugh, or smile. If you must sneeze or cough, that is fine, but try to minimize noise.

Clean clothes: Your clothes should be clean and should cover the body. For boys, clothes should cover the body at least from the navel to the knees. For girls, clothes should cover the body from the neck to the ankle, and to the wrist. The head is covered, but the face can remain uncovered. Clothes should not be transparent. Avoid any clothing that has pictures of people, animals, or offensive writings.

Clean place: You should find a clean place to make your salāh. A prayer rug is not necessary. A prayer rug should always be clean, so it ensures a clean place while you are praying.

Direction to face: You will be facing *Qiblah*, which is the direction of the Ka'bah in Makkah.

Time: *Fard* (compulsory) prayers are performed at the proper and appointed time. It is preferable to perform the prayer as soon as the *Adhān* (call to prayer) is announced.

Mental preparation: We begin the prayer with full mental and physical attention. During *salāh*, we are worshipping and talking directly to Allāh, therefore, we must show total attention. Avoid any place or object that diverts your full attention.

What is a raka'ah? Each salāh can be divided into cycles of physical postures or raka'at. Each raka'ah involves the positions of *qiyam* (standing), *ruku* (bowing), *sujud* (prostration), *jalsa* (sitting), another *sujud* (prostration), and associated recitations. The following chart shows the specified number of raka'at for the five daily salāh. Some variation in the number of Sunnah prayer exists among the madhhab.

	Sunnah raka'at before Fard raka'at	Fard raka'at	Sunnah raka'at after Fard raka'at
Fajr	2	2	
Dhuhr	4	4	2
'Asr	4	4	
Maghrib		3	2
'Isha	4	4	2, then 3 (wajib)

Description for a salah of two raka'at:

The following description of steps is for a salāh with two raka'at (for example, the Fard prayer of Fajr). At the end of this description, there are brief notes about how to perform three or four raka'at of salāh.

Step 1
(Figures above)

When you stand up for salāh, make an intention to perform the salāh for the sake of Allāh. Say to yourself (in any language) that you intend to offer this *Salāh* (*Fajr, Dhuhr, Asr, Maghrib,* or *Isha*), *Fard, Sunnat,* or *Witr,* and the number of raka'ahs (example—"I intend to offer two *raka'ah* of *Fard, Fajr* prayer for Allāh").

Position: *Qiyam.* You are standing upright. Raise both hands up to the ears (palms facing the *Qiblah* —body facing the direction of the Ka'bah).

What to say: *"Allāhu Akbar"* (Allāh is the Greatest).

Step 2
(Figures on the right)

Position: Place your left hand over your belly, place your right hand on top of the left hand, and grip the wrist of the left hand.

What to say:

1. *"Subhanaka Allāhumma wa bihamdika, wa tabārakasmuka, wa ta'āla jadduka, wa lā ilāha ghairuka."* (This part is known as *thana.* It means "Glory be to you, O Allāh, and praise to You. Blessed be Your Name, exalted be Your Majesty and Glory. There is no god but You").

2. *"A'ūdu billāhi mina ash-Shaytānir rajim."* (I seek the protection of Allāh against Shaitān, the condemned.)

3. *"Bismillāhir rahmānir rahīm."* (In the Name of Allāh, Most Gracious, Most Merciful.)

4. Now recite Sūrah Al-Fātihah now. We must recite Sūrah Al-Fātihah during each raka'ah. A salāh is not valid if Sūrah Al-Fātihah is not recited.

"Al humdu li-llahi rabbi-l 'alamīn. Ar-rahmāni-r rahīm. Māliki yawmi-d dīn. Iyyāka na'budu wa iyyāka Nāsta'īn. Ihdina-s sirāta-l mustaqīm. Sirātal ladhīna an'amta 'alaihim, ghairil maghdūbi 'alaihim, wa la-d dāllīn. (Āmīn)."

(The Praise belongs to Allāh, The Rabb of all the worlds; the Rahman; the Rahim. Malik of the Day of Judgment. You alone do we serve, and to You alone we seek help. Guide us on the Right Path—the path of those upon whom You have bestowed favors; not of those upon whom wrath is brought down, nor those gone astray.)

5. After reciting sūrah Fātihah, we now recite any short sūrah or a few verses from the Qur'ān. This additional recitation of a part of the Qur'ān is done during the first two raka'ah only. It is always good to memorize as many sūrah as you can, so you can recite them during your salāh.

What to say: "Samia Allāhu liman hamidah." (Allāh listens to him who praises Him.)

Position: In qiyam position.

What to say: "Rabbanā wa laka al hamd." (Our Rabb, praise be for You only.)

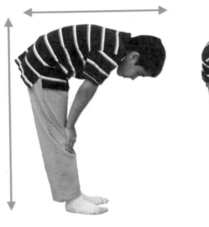

Step 3   (Figures above)

What to say: "Allāhu Akbar."

Position: This position is called ruku. Bow with your back perpendicular to your legs. Place your hands on your knees. Do not bend the knees.

What to say: "Subhana rabbiyal 'Adhīm." (say this three times.) (Glorified is my Rabb, the Great.)

Step 5   (Figure above)

What to say: While moving to the next position of sujud, say "Allāhu Akbar."

Position: This position is sujud. Place both of your knees on the floor. Try not to move the position of your feet, that is, do not move your feet away from the position of qiyam. After placing the knees, then you will place your two hands on the floor with palms touching the floor. Do not glide your hands on the floor. Your elbow is not on the floor. Your hands should be sufficiently apart to leave room for your head. Now place your forehead on the floor. Both your nose and forehead should touch the floor. Your hands are on the side of your head. Your stomach will not touch the floor. You should be the most humble in this position.

The most powerful part of our body is our brain, the site of our intelligence. We submit our full selves, with full understanding, to Almighty Allāh. We realize that our strength, power, wealth, and everything that we have is from Allāh. To confirm this physical and spiritual humility, we will repeat the sujud again in Step 7.

What to say: "Subhana rabbiyal A'ala." (say this three times.) (Glory be to Allāh, the Exalted.)

Step 4   (Figures below)

While going back to qiyam (upright) position,

Step 6 (Figures above)

The next position is *jalsa.*

What to say: While moving to the *jalsa* position, say "*Allāhu Akbar.*"

Position: To move to *jalsa* position, rise from *sujud.* First you will raise your head off the floor, then you will raise your hands. Now you are sitting on the floor— this posture is called *jalsa.*

What to say: "*Rabbi-ghfir lī wa rhamnī.*" (O my Rabb, forgive me and have mercy on me.)

Step 7 (Figure above)

We will repeat the *sujud* again. Every *raka'ah* has two *sujud.*

What to say: While moving to the position of *sujud,* say "*Allāhu Akbar.*"

Position: *Sujud.* Place your palms on the floor, and then your forehead. Both the nose and the forehead should be touching the floor.

What to say: "*Subhāna rabbiyal A'ala.*" (say this three times.) (Glory to Allāh, the Exalted.)

This completes one raka'ah

Step 8 (Figures above)

Rise to *qiyam* (standing) position. The movement should be in a systematic, graceful manner. First you will raise your forehead from the floor, then you will raise your hands and then you will raise your knees. Try not to move your feet, that is, the position of your feet should be the same as it was during the first *raka'ah.*

What to say: While moving to the position of *qiyam,* say "*Allāhu Akbar.*"

Position: You are standing upright. Hold the left hand with the right hand on top.

What to say: Sūrah Al-Fātihah, then any short sūrah or a few verses from the Qur'ān.

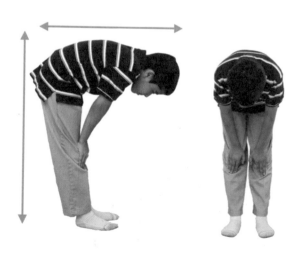

Step 9

(Figures in the previous page)

What to say: "*Allāhu Akbar.*"

Position: *Ruku.* Bow with your back perpendicular to your legs. Place your hands on your knees.

What to say: "*Subhāna rabbiyal 'Adhīm.*" (say it this three times.)

Step 10

(Figures above)

Position: While moving back to *qiyam* (standing) position,

What to say: "*Sami'a Allāhu liman hamidah.*"

Position: In *qiyam* position. You are upright.

What to say: "*Rabbanā wa lakal hamd.*"

Step 11

(Figure below)

What to say: While moving to the next position of *sujud*, say "*Allāhu Akbar.*"

Position: *Sujud.* Follow the same sequence in Step 5.

What to say: "*Subhāna Rabbiyal A'ala.*" (say this three times.)

Step 12

(Figures above)

What to say: While moving to the next position of *jalsa*, say "*Allāhu Akbar.*"

Position: Rise from the *sujud* position. Now you are sitting in *jalsa* position.

What to say: "'*Rabbi-ghfir lī wa rhamnī*" (O my Rabb, forgive me and have Mercy on me.)

Step 13

(Figure above)

What to say: While moving to the next position of sujud, say "*Allāhu Akbar.*"

Position: *Sujud.* First place your hands and then your forehead on the floor.

What to say: "*Subhāna Rabbiyal A'ala.*" (say this three times.)

Step 14

(Figures in the next page)

What to say: While going to the next position of *jalsa*, say "*Allāhu Akbar.*"

Position: Rise from the *sujud* position. Now you are sitting on *jalsa* position.

What to say: You will say *Tashahud, Durūd,* and a short prayer as follows:

"At-tahiyātu lillahi was-salawātu wattaiyibātu. Assalāmu 'alayka ayyuhan-nabiyu wa rahmat-ullāhi wa barakātuhu. Assalāmu 'alainā wa 'ala 'ibadi-llāhis-sālihīn. Ashhadu an lā ilāha illallāhu wa ashhadu anna Muhammadan 'abduhu wa rasūluhu."

(All these salutations, prayers and nice things are for Allāh. Peace be on you, O Prophet, and the blessings of Allāh, and His grace. Peace on us and on all the righteous servants of Allāh. I bear witness that none but Allāh is worthy of worship, and I bear witness that Muhammad is the servant and messenger of Allāh.) This is known as *Tashahud.*

Position: Raise your right index finger, so it is pointing upward, while reciting the last part of this prayer.

Next you will recite the *Durūd.*

"Allāhumma salli 'ala Muhammadin wa 'ala āli Muhummadin, kamā sallayta 'ala Ibrāhima, wa ala āli Ibrāhima, innaka hamidun majid. Allāhumma barik 'ala Muhammadin wa 'ala āli Muhummadin, kama barakta ala Ibrāhima, wa 'ala āli Ibrāhīm, innaka hamīdun majīd."

(O Allāh, send your Mercy on Muhammad and his posterity as you sent Your mercy on Ibrāhīm and his posterity. You are the Most Praised, The Most Glorious. O Allāh, send your Blessings on Muhammad and his posterity as you have blessed Ibrāhīm and his posterity. You are the Most praised, The Most Glorious.)

Now you may add a short prayer, such as:

"Rabbanā ātinā fi-d dunyā hasanatan wa fi-l ākhirati hasanatan, wa qinā 'adhāban nār."

(Our Rabb, give us the good of this world, and good in the Hereafter, and save us from the chastisement of Fire.)

Step 15　　　　(Figure above left)

Position: Slowly turn your head and face right. This is called *salam.*

What to say: *"As-salāmu 'alaikum wa rahma-tullāh."* (Peace and mercy of Allāh be on you).

Step 16　　　　(Figure above right)

Position: Slowly turn your head and face left. This is called salam.

What to say: *"As-salāmu 'alaikum wa rahma-tullāh."*

This completes the two raka'at of salāh.

How to pray three raka'ats (Maghrib)

In order to perform a three-raka'at Salāh, use all the postures and prayers up to step 13.

In step 14, recite up to *"At-tahiyātu lillahi was-salawātu wattaiyibātu. Assalāmu 'alayka ayyuhan-nabiyu wa rahmatullāhi wa barakātuhu. Assalāmu 'ainā wa 'ala 'ibadi-llāhis-sālihīn. Ashhadu an lā ilāha illallāhu wa ashhadu anna Muhammadan 'abduhu wa rasūluhu."* This is known as *Tashahud*.

After saying *"Allāhu akbar,"* return to the *qiyam* position, step 8. This time recite only *Al-Fātihah*, (in step 8), but do not recite any sūrah or part of the Qur'ān. All prayers and postures are the same as shown in step 9–16.

How to pray four raka'ats (Dhuhr, 'Asr and 'Isha)

In order to perform a four-raka'at prayer, use all the postures and prayers up to step 13.

In Step 14, only the prayer of *Tashahud* will be recited, and the *qiyam* position, in step 8, will be resumed.

In step 8, only *Al-Fātihah* will be recited without adding any sūrah. Steps 8–13 complete the third raka'ah. The *qiyam* position in step 8 will be resumed.

In step 8, only *Al-Fātihah* will be recited, without adding any sūrah. Steps 8–16, completes the fourth raka'ah.

From the Qur'an

...keep up the salāt, as salāt controls indecent and unacceptable behaviors... *(Sūrah Al-'Ankabūt, 29:45)*

Take care to do your salāt, praying in the best way, and stand before Allāh with full devotion. *(Sūrah Al-Baqarah, 2:238)*

Summary of Prayer Postures

Standing for salāt facing the direction of Ka'bah.

Front and lateral view

Raising hands for takbir. Folding them back to recite sūrah.

Bending position for ruku.

Front and lateral view

Raising from ruku.

Performing sujud.

Sitting down from sujud, jalsa position.

Front, lateral and back view

Second sujud from jalsa position.

At the end of 2nd raka'at, sitting down after 2nd sujud to recite tashahud.

Completing salāt—turning face first to the right and then to the left.

Test Your Knowledge - 1

(All questions are based on the lessons taught in this book.)

1. What is the name of the cave where Muhammad (S) first received revelation?

2. What is the Arabic term for showing patience?

3. Before marriage, where did Khadījah (ra) send Muhammad (S) to conduct business on her behalf?

4. After his birth, where was infant Muhammad (S) sent with a nurse-mother?

5. What is the meaning of the word jāhiliyyah?

6. Which prophet was born in the "Year of the Elephant"?

7. In which language is the Jewish book, the Tawrat written?

8. What is the meaning of Allāh's name Al-Quddus?

9. Who was sleeping on the bed when the Quraish men came to kill Muhammad (S)?

10. In which year did our Nabi Muhammad (S) liberate Makkah?

11. Which Eid is celebrated on the first day of Shawwal?

12. Who was 'Ali's (r) wife?

13. Which Khalīfah defeated a person who falsely claimed to be a prophet?

14. In 628 C.E., which treaty was signed between the Muslims and the Quraish?

15. In which year did Prophet Muhammad (S) pass away?

Answer:
1. Cave Hira
2. Sabr
3. Syria
4. Tā'if
5. Ignorance
6. Muhammad (S)
7. Hebrew
8. The Holy
9. 'Ali
10. In 630 C.E.
11. Eid al-Fitr
12. Fātimah
13. Abu Bakr (r)
14. Treaty of Hudaibiyah
15. 632 C.E. or 10 A.H.

Test Your Knowledge - 2

(All questions are based on the lessons taught in this book.)

1. During which prophet's time did the queen of Sheba live?

2. Which sūrah contains the first five verses revealed to our Nabi Muhammad (S)?

3. Who was the nurse-mother who cared for infant Muhammad (S)?

4. What is the meaning of Allāh's name Al-Salām?

5. What is the English name of Zabūr—the book revealed to Dāwūd (A)?

6. From which country did Abrahah come to destroy the Ka'bah?

7. Who was the first guardian of Muhammad (S) after his mother died?

8. Which Christian monk said Muhammad (S) would become a prophet when he grew up?

9. What is the name of the two pledges taken by the people of Madīnah?

10. What was the first battle Muslims fought after they migrated to Madīnah?

11. On which day in the month of Dhul Hajj do we celebrate Eid al-Adha?

12. After infant Mūsā (A) was rescued from the river, who was engaged to feed him and raise him?

13. Which prophet's people killed a she-camel by cutting the back of her ankle?

14. What two false hopes did Shaitān give to Adam (A) if he ate from the tree?

15. What is the term for the chain of narrators at the beginning of a hadīth?

Answer:
1. Sulaimān 2. Sūrah 'Alaq 3. Halīmah 4. Peace 5. Psalms 6. Yemen 7. Abdul Muttalib 8. Bahīrah 9. Pledges of 'Aqabah 10. Battle of Badr 11. On the tenth day 12. His own mother 13. Sālih (A) 14. That he would become an angel or live forever 15. Isnad

Test Your Knowledge - 3

(All questions are based on the lessons taught in this book.)

1. Whose daughter's name was 'A'ishah?

2. What is the term for the people of Madīnah who helped the Muslims?

3. Which sūrah describes elephants trying to destroy the Ka'bah?

4. Who was Nabi Muhammad's (S) guardian after his grandfather died?

5. During the hijrah to Madīnah, who went with Muhammad (S)?

6. What was the second battle the Muslims fought after they migrated to Madīnah?

7. Who was the second Khalīfah?

8. Which Khalīfah circulated official copies of the Qur'ān?

9. Who was the husband of Rasūlullāh's (S) daughter Fātimah (r)?

10. Who was the prophet for the people of 'Ad?

11. What is the first month of the Islamic calendar?

12. Sulaimān (A) brought something from Sheba to his kingdom without the knowledge of the queen. What was the item?

13. How long was Mūsā (A) asked to live in Madyan after he agreed to get married?

14. Who was the Khalīfah of the Muslim world immediately before 'Ali (r)?

15. Which would-be Khalīfa wanted to kill his sister for becoming a Muslim, but she helped him become a Muslim?

Answer:
1. Abu Bakr
2. Ansars
3. Sūrah Al-Fīl
4. Abū Tālib
5. Abu Bakr
6. Battle of Uhud
7. 'Umar
8. 'Uthman
9. 'Ali
10. Hūd
11. Muharram
12. Her throne
13. Eight to ten years
14. Uthman
15. 'Umar

Test Your Knowledge - 4

(All questions are based on the lessons taught in this book.)

1. To which place did Mūsā (A) run after killing an Egyptian?

2. When Mūsā (A) returned to Egypt, which prophet went with him?

3. What is the name of the cave where Muhammad (S) hid during hijrah to Madīnah?

4. Which Khalīfah established the Islamic calendar starting from the date of Hijrah?

5. Who was the prophet for the people of Thamūd?

6. Which queen entered the palace of Sulaimān (A) by walking over glass slabs?

7. What is the name of the most famous collector of hadīth?

8. How old was 'Ali when Muhammad (S) became a prophet of Allāh?

9. What sign did prophet Sālih (A) provide for his people?

10. Who was the Khalīfah of the Muslim world immediately before 'Umar al-Khattāb (r)?

11. How many years of peace were agreed upon in the Treaty of Hudaibiyah?

12. Which battle could the Muslims not win because the archers ignored Rasūlullāh's (S) instruction?

13. A cousin of Khadījah (ra) assured Muhammad (S) that he was a messenger of Allāh. What was the cousin's name?

14. In the year of 'Aml al-Fīl, who came to Makkah with bad intentions?

15. The Old Testament and New Testament are parts of which book?

Answer:
1. Madyan
2. His brother, Hārūn
3. Thawr
4. 'Umar
5. Sālih
6. Bilqis
7. Bukhārī
8. Ten years old
9. A she-camel
10. Abu Bakr
11. Ten years
12. Battle of Uhud
13. Waraqah
14. Abrahah
15. The Bible

Outline of Curriculum—Grades 1, 2, and 3

Each year the curriculum begins with a few topics on Allāh, the Qur'ān, Rasūlullāh (S), the Hadīth, or Sunnah. In the early years, the emphasis is placed on the 5 pillars, and each year, this emphasis increases. Each year, a history of some of the prophets is introduced in an age-appropriate manner. Several lessons are devoted to Islamic manners, values, and morals so that children grow up with a good understanding of Islamic culture. Each lesson includes a homework assignment.

Week	1st Grade	2nd Grade	3rd Grade
1	Allāh	Allāh the Creator	What Does Allāh Do
2	Islam	Blessings of Allāh	Some Names of Allāh
3	Our Faith	The Qur'ān	Allāh: the Merciful
4	Muhammad (S)	Muhammad (S)	Allāh: the Judge
5	The Qur'ān	Sunnah and Hadīth	We Are Muslims
6	An exam is recommended this week		
7	5 Pillars of Islam	5 Pillars of Islam	Other Names of the Qur'ān
8	Shahādah	Shahādah	Hadith
9	Salāt and Wūdū	Salāt	Shahādah
10	Fasting	Sawm	Types of salāt
11	Zakah	Charity	Why Do Salāt
12	An exam is recommended this week		
13	Hajj	Hajj	Sawm
14	Saying Bismillāh	Wūdū	Charity
15	Angels	Four Khalīfas	Hajj
16	Shaitān	Ibrāhīm (A)	Prophet (S) in Makkah
17	Adam (A)	Ya'qūb (A) and Yūsuf (A)	Prophet (S) in Madinah
18	Nūh (A)	Mūsā (A) and Harun (A)	How Rasul (S) Treated Others
19	An exam is recommended this week		
20	Ibrāhīm (A)	Yūnus (A)	Ismā'īl (A) and Ishāq (A)
21	Mūsā (A)	Angels	Dāwūd (A)
22	'Isā (A)	Food That We May Eat	'Isā (A)
23	Makkah and Madinah	Truthfulness	Being Kind
24	Good Manners	Kindness	Forgiveness
25	Kindness and Sharing	Respect	Good Deeds
26	An exam is recommended this week		
27	Allāh Rewards Good Works	Responsibility	Cleanliness
28	Respect	Obedience	Right Path
29	Forgiveness	Cleanliness	A Muslim Family
30	Love of Allāh	Honesty	Perseverance
31	Eid	Day of Judgment and Hereafter	Punctuality
32	Thanking Allāh	Muslims from Different Nations	Jinn
33	An exam is recommended this week		

Outline of Curriculum—Grades 4, 5, and 6

By 5th grade, a summarized biography of Rasūlullāh (S) is completed, including an understanding of the events that shaped his life and early Islam. By 6th grade, students will have studied the biography of most of the prominent prophets at least once. At this stage, students will have learned all the fundamental principles and key concepts of Islam. Even if the students do not enroll in weekend schools after 6th grade, they will have gained significant age-appropriate knowledge about Islam.

Week	4th Grade	5th Grade	6th Grade
1	Rewards of Allāh	Allāh: Our Sole Master	Attributes of Allāh
2	Discipline of Allāh	Why Should We Worship Allāh	The Promise of Allāh
3	Some Names of Allāh	Revelation of the Qur'ān	Objectives of the Qur'ān
4	Books of Allāh	Characteristics of Prophets	Compilation of the Qur'ān
5	Pre-Islamic Arabia	Battle of Badr	Previous Scriptures and the Qur'ān
6	An exam is recommended this week		
7	The Year of the Elephant	Battle of Uhud	The Importance of Shahādah
8	Early Life of Muhammad (S)	Battle of Trench	Hadīth, Compilation, Narrators
9	Life Before Becoming a Nabi	Hudaibiyah Treaty	Nūh (A)
10	First Revelation	Conquest of Makkah	Tālūt, Jālūt, and Dāwūd (A)
11	Makkan Period	Adam (A)	Dāwūd (A) and Sulaimān (A)
12	An exam is recommended this week		
13	Pledges of Aqaba	Ibrāhīm (A) and His Arguments	Sulaimān (A) and Queen of Saba
14	Hijrat to Madinah	Ibrāhīm (A) and Idols	Mūsā (A) and Fir'awn
15	Madīnan Period	Luqmān (A) and His Teachings	Israelites After Their Rescue
16	Victory of Makkah	Yūsuf (A)—Childhood and Life in Aziz's Home	Mūsā (A) and Khidir
17	Abū Bakr (R)	Yūsuf (A)—Life in Prison and His Dream Interpretation	'Isā (A) and Maryam (ra)
18	'Umar al-Khattāb (R)	Yūsuf (A)—Dream Fulfills	Khadījah (ra)
19	An exam is recommended this week		
20	'Uthmān ibn 'Affan (R)	Ayyūb (A)	'A'ishah (ra)
21	'Ali Ibn Abu Tālib (R)	Zakariyyāh (A) and Yahyā (A)	Fātimah (ra)
22	Compilers of Hadith	Maryam	Al-Qiyamah: The Awakening
23	Shaitān's Mode of Operation	Major Masjid in the World	Rūh and Nafs
24	Hūd (A)	Upholding Truth	The Angels and Jinn
25	Sālih (A)	Responsibility and Punctuality	Shaitān: The Invisible Enemy
26	An exam is recommended this week		
27	Mūsā (A)	My Mind, My Body	Taqwā
28	Sulaimān (A)	Kindness and Forgiveness	My Friend Is Muslim Now
29	Truthfulness	Middle Path	Friendship: With People of the Same and Opposite Gender
30	Perseverance	Significance of Salāt	Reading Salāt vs Performing Salāt
31	Day of Judgment	Significance of Fasting	Muslims Around the World
32	'Eid and Its Significance	Zakāt and Sadaqah	People of Other Faith
33	An exam is recommended this week		

Outline of Curriculum—Grades 7, 8, and 9

In these grades, the application of knowledge is gradually emphasized by using carefully selected topics. Details about some of the prophets are introduced to highlight the abiding morals in their lives. In 8th grade, several battles and early Muslim struggles are discussed in detail. Increased depth and emphasis of the lessons require focused attention from students. Age-appropriate moral lessons, for example, gossip, friendship, peer pressure, dating, indecency, encouraging good and forbidding evil, and so forth are covered.

Week	7th Grade	8th Grade	9th Grade
1	Why Islam? what is Islam?	Divine Names	Signs of Allāh in nature
2	The Qur'ān—other names	Objectives of the Qur'ān	Pondering the Qur'ān
3	Seeking the Forgiveness of Allāh —Istighfar	Hadīth	Preservation and Compilation of the Qur'ān
4	Allāh: Angry or Kind	Madhhab	Ibadat—Easy Ways to Do It
5	Islamic Greetings	Hope, Hopefulness, Hopelessness	Why Human Beings Are Superior
6	An exam is recommended this week		
7	Ādam (A)	Trial	Is Islam a Violent Religion?
8	'Ad and Thamūd	Friends and Friendship	Peer Pressure
9	Stories of Ibrāhīm (A) - I	Friendship With Non-Muslims	Choices We Make
10	Stories of Ibrāhīm (A) - II	Dating in Islam	Dating in Islam
11	Sacrifice of Ibrāhīm (A)	Duties Toward Parents	Alcohol and Gambling
12	An exam is recommended this week		
13	Lūt (A)	Islam for Middle School Students	Permitted and Prohibited Food
14	Yūsuf (A)—The Story of Overcoming Temptation	Battle of Badr	Food of the People of the Book
15	The Dwellers of the Cave	Battle of Uhud	Khadījah (ra)
16	Dhul Qurnain	Banu Qaynuka	Prophet's (S) Multiple Marriages
17	Abū Sufyān	Banu Nadir	Marriage to Zainab (ra)
18	Khālid Ibn Walīd (R)	Battle of Khandaq	The Prophet: A Great Army General
19	An exam is recommended this week		
20	How to Achieve Success	Banu Qurayzah	God's Chosen People
21	The Character of the Prophets	Surah Al-Ahzāb on the Battle of Khandaq	Mūsā's Personality
22	The Prophet's (S) Marriages	Hudaibiyah Treaty	Prophecy of Muhammad(S) in Bible
23	Purification	Tabūk Expedition	Essentials of Salah
24	Permitted and Prohibited	Farewell Pilgrimage	Muslims in North America
25	Lailatul Qadr	Performance of Hajj	Life Cycle of Truth
26	An exam is recommended this week		
27	Fasting During Ramadan	Paradise and Hell	How Ramadan Makes Us Better
28	My Family is Muslim Now	Finality of Prophethood	Indecency
29	Amr Bil Ma'rūf	Origin and History of Shī'ah	Allegations Against the Prophet (S)
30	Guard Your Tongue	Ummayad Dynasty	Family Values
31	Lessons from Past Civilizations	Abbasid Dynasty	Shariah
32	Science in the Qur'ān	Permitted and Prohibited Food	Justice in Islam
33	An exam is recommended this week		

Outline of Curriculum—Grades 10, 11 and 12

In 10th, 11th — 12th grades, Islamic topics increasingly prepare youths to fine-tune their spiritual and social lives. Significant issues that have real-life implications are introduced. The application of knowledge continues to be emphasized. The lessons in 11—12 grade book strongly promote application of core Islamic knowledge. This is done through carefully selected topics. All the lessons teach Islamic belief and understanding based on the Qur'ān and authentic Hadith.

Week	10th Grade	11th —12th Grade
1	History of the Word "Allāh"	Islam
2	An Analysis of Fātihah	Muslim
3	Fātiha vs. The Lord's Prayer	Shahādah
4	Muhkam Mutashabihat Verses	Belief in Allāh
5	Al-Asr—The Formula of Success	Belief in the Angels
6	An exam is recommended this week	
7	Qur'ānic Calligraphy	Belief in the Revealed Books
8	The Bible and the Qur'ān	Belief in the Messengers
9	The Ten Commandments and Islam	Belief in the Hereafter
10	Adam and Eve in the Garden	Life's Ultimate Purpose
11	Women in the Qur'ān	Wealth Is The "Driver"
12	An exam is recommended this week	
13	Muslim Family	The "Driver" Within Us
14	The Status of Women in Islam	When Allāh Seems Distant
15	Marriage to Non-Muslims	Tawakkul: Trust in Allāh
16	Marrying Four Women	Du'ā: How Does Allāh Respond?
17	Difficult Questions on Marriage	A Heart for Allāh
18	Who is Khalifah on the Earth	Controlling Your Thoughts
19	An exam is recommended this week	
20	False Piety	Maintaining a Relationship
21	Superstition	The Power of Forgiveness
22	Do Not Transgress Limits	Reading the Qur'ān
23	Secular and Religious Duties	Lower Your Gaze
24	Racism in Islam	Ā'ishah (ra): The Child Bride
25	Principles of Islamic Economy	Afraid to Think, Forbidden to Ask
26	An exam is recommended this week	
27	Public Finance in Early Islam	"Strike" in Sūrah An-Nisā'
28	Islamic Architecture	The Myth About the Satanic Verse
29	Islam in Spain and Portugal	How Jesus Became Christ
30	Independent project	Rūh and Nafs
31	Independent project	Independent project
32	Independent project	Independent project
33	An exam is recommended this week	

Other useful books for a complete teaching system

Arabic Writing Workbook

128 pages $10.00

My Islamic Coloring Book

136 pages $10.00

My Islamic Activity Book

160 pages $12.00

Beginners 5-Pillars of Islam Activity Book

96 pages $10.00

Juz Amma For School Students (with transliteration)

216 pages $13.00

Juz Amma For School Students (without transliteration)

216 pages $13.00

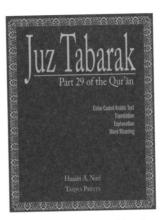

Juz Tabarak: Part 29 of the Qur'ān

200 pages $13.00

Beginners Arabic Reading

36 pages $6.00

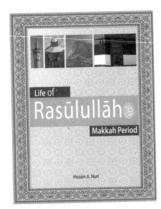

Life of Rasūlullāh (S): Makkah Period

176 pages $13.00

Life of Rasūlullāh (Ṡ): Madinah Period

196 pages $13.00

Quiz Book on Islam: For All Levels of Expertise

160 pages $10.00

Tajweed Made Easy

100 pages $12.00